A DEDICATED LIFE

Journalism, Justice, and a Chance for Every Child

DAVID LAWRENCE JR.

The Children's Movement Founder

BOOKS & BOOKS
PRESS

For permission requests, please contact the publisher at:
Books & Books Press
Mango Publishing Group
2850 Douglas Road, 3rd Floor
Coral Gables, FL 33134 USA
info@mango.bz

For special orders, quantity sales, course adoptions and corporate sales, please email the publisher at sales@mango.bz. For trade and wholesale sales, please contact Ingram Publisher Services at customer.service@ingramcontent.com or +1.800.509.4887.

A Dedicated Life: Journalism, Justice, and a Chance for Every Child

Library of Congress Cataloging
ISBN: (paperback) 978-1-63353-818-4, (ebook) 978-1-63353-819-1
Library of Congress Control Number: 2018941609
BISAC category code: BIO026000—BIOGRAPHY & AUTOBIOGRAPHY / Personal Memoirs

Printed in the United States of America

*For Roberta and our children and their families—
and everyone's child and everyone's family.*

*For Jane and Gerald Katcher, and Lawton Chiles.
It wouldn't have happened without them.*

CONTENTS

FOREWORD

By Gov. Jeb Bush

Throughout my time in government and politics, I have been blessed to meet thousands of passionate advocates for children—teachers, parents, community aid workers, health care professionals and philanthropists—but few have been as singularly committed to transforming the quality of life for all young children as David Lawrence.

This special book is the story of a good man who has lived an impressive, fascinating, full life dedicated to his family, his profession, his faith and his service to others, especially the youngest and most vulnerable among us.

Following in his father's footsteps—both being inductees into the Florida Newspaper Hall of Fame—David pursued a career in journalism. He was a journalist's journalist, during an era when the truth was not subjective, and when fairness and accuracy were prized above all else.

From his start at the *St. Petersburg Times* to his time as an editor at *The Washington Post* to his career-capping leadership as publisher of the *Miami Herald*, David brought integrity to the field, and to Florida journalism in particular. As such, I hope readers and newsmen and newswomen pay close attention to David's advice regarding the future of journalism. The industry sure could use it.

As an adopted son of Miami, I'm proud that it was our hometown that ignited and fostered David's second career—that as a leading advocate for early childhood development and school readiness. David retired as publisher of the *Herald* the year I took office as governor of Florida, in 1999. It is with joy and appreciation that I had the opportunity to work with him on a range of education and community issues during the course of my administration and in the years following.

David and I share a philosophy on education that is based on two simple principles—(1) every life is a gift from God and (2) every child can learn. When this basic premise is embraced, it is a good start to building consensus and finding broad-based solutions.

Within months of his retirement from the *Herald*, David was able to convene five thousand Miami community leaders for a major summit tackling the most pressing issues facing our youngest citizens and their families, chiefly their early care and development. David's efforts quickly grew into a statewide movement that eventually culminated in a successful 2002 constitutional amendment campaign to make voluntary prekindergarten (VPK) available to all four-year-olds in Florida.

Today, Florida's VPK program is the largest universal prekindergarten program in the nation and the largest school-choice program in America, with 175,000 students participating. We are one of only four states to offer such a program to all four-year-olds. As chair of The Children's Movement of Florida, David continues his advocacy for early childhood education today and remains a leading state and national advocate on these issues.

It's an honor to call David not just a friend, but a mentor on these critical policy issues. I hope his story inspires many more to follow his path.

David has said his "lifelong hunger has been for fairness, for justice, for decency, for love." Without a doubt, he has achieved these goals and more. Our state and countless Floridians, young and old, are better because he did.

~~~

A politician, businessman, and public education reformer, Jeb Bush served as Florida's 43rd governor from 1999 to 2007 and as a presidential candidate in 2016.

FOREWORD

By U.S. Sen. Bob Graham

R eading David Lawrence's autobiography, you will learn a lot—from disemboweling chickens on an upstate New York farm, to the evolution of Miami from *Miami Vice* to a culturally and economically international city, to the travails of contemporary journalism. Reading this book is like listening to an old friend telling engaging stories while encouraging you to join the conversation.

Dave's successful career in journalism is a story of the roller coaster of the American newspaper from the halcyon days of post-World War II to the dramatic changes and decline of today. For more than forty years, Dave was a journalist, rising from co-editor of his high school newspaper to editor or publisher of several of America's most distinguished newspapers. At each, he inspired the highest standards of journalism built upon a deep immersion into the communities these newspapers served.

While engaged in an intense professional life, he and his wife Bobbie raised five charming and talented children. (In a spirit of full disclosure, one of those, the middle child, Amanda, was a valuable member of my Senate staff and legislative director during the final months. She turned off the lights in our Hart Senate Office Building office when I retired, and we left the building together for the final time.)

But the most lasting impression you'll have will be of a highly principled man applying his talents and values in a transitioning America. Ultimately, he elects to transfer his lifelong fascination with journalism to civic advocacy for early childhood learning.

As one who has been asked, "What are you going to do for the rest of your life?" I recognize the answer to be among the most important self-defining phases of life: Maybe, nothing at all. Perhaps, a continuation of your former career, albeit at a reduced level. Or something that your life experience has prepared you for, but which other demands precluded you from pursuing.

At the age of fifty-six, Dave decided to embark on his new path with, in his words, "newly energized purposefulness: that every child have a real chance to succeed." He motivated a mosaic of men and women to join his cause, established an institutional framework in which they could gather, and played a crucial role in passing a state constitutional amendment enshrining the centrality of early learning to a lifetime of success.

How he describes using the passion, persistence, and skills of civic engagement to accomplish these building blocks to success is worth the price of the book. To cement and broaden those achievements, Dave created a movement that has converted aspiration to reality and has, is, and will enrich the lives of thousands of the youngest Floridians. He has brought life to the truism of Frederick Douglass: "It is easier to build strong children than to repair broken men."

This book tells the full story. Not bad as a retirement project!

~~~

Bob Graham is a veteran politician and author who served as Florida's 38th governor from 1979 to 1987, as a U.S. senator from Florida from 1987 to 2005, and as a presidential candidate in 2003.

PREFACE

"Do all the good you can. By all the means you can. In all the ways you can. To all the people you can. As long as ever you can."
—Eighteenth-century theologian John Wesley

Stop and smell the roses, people tell me. Slow down, they say. I can't. Or won't. I am, to be sure, driven, and have been all my life. I wish I were less so. But it seems too late now to change the likely unchangeable.

What, after all, would I want to change? Been in love with the same person for more than a half-century. Raised five children, all really good people. Made possible our first grandchild's baptism at the Vatican. Dined with Queen Elizabeth II and, on another occasion, sat alongside Margaret Thatcher. (Neither was eager for an intimate, revealing conversation!) Met every President—before, during or after his term—from Richard Nixon through Donald Trump. Dined twice at the White House.

Rode through the *barrios* of Lima with Peruvian President Fujimori at the wheel driving maniacally. Honored by Billy Graham. Serenaded as a surprise on my forty-fifth birthday by Patti Page singing her 1950s hit, "The Tennessee Waltz," the first song I can remember, at age eight. Had an audience with Pope John Paul II, who wanted to know about Miami and Cuba.

Asked questions in fifty-six countries—questions about leadership, the future, politics, geography. Saw the sights from the Grand Canyon to the Great Wall, Petra to the Pyramids. Traveled to places where I never saw a tourist—Bangladesh, for instance, where my wife and I sat on a carpet atop dirt in a village square and talked about micro-lending with fifteen women, and the Democratic Republic of Congo where I interviewed child rape victims.

My first immediate family was close and strong—father, mother, and nine children. We loved each other, but never demonstratively so. "Love" wasn't a word much used in our home. A third of a century ago, as my father lay dying from liver cancer in a Tallahassee hospital, I flew down from Detroit to see him and my mother. As I was getting ready to depart and leaned down to kiss him on his forehead—he would die two weeks later—he said to me: "I want you to know how proud your mother and I are of you."

However wonderful that compliment, it was not what I most wanted to hear. I wished he could have said: "I love you." But that was not in our family's "culture." It is now. Ever since, I have made it my personal practice to tell my children "I love you" every time I speak with them, and their families and, now, with so many other people. Everyone needs love. We all need to be comfortable enough with ourselves to tell people just that.

Speaking of which, I've been in love, sentimentally and deeply so, with the same woman for more than fifty years. I love Roberta Phyllis Fleischman Lawrence even more today than I did more than a half-century ago—and I did love her then, too. I have the remarkable advantage of being married to someone who has put up with me—with my schedule, with my work ethic, with my occasional bad moods and exhaustion. I have been asked many times, "What is the secret of your long and loving marriage?" I respond, and smile: "Because she knew from the very beginning—and accepted—that I was a driven idiot!" That "very beginning" came when we were both nineteen.

Roberta is the greatest blessing of my life. I call her several times a day, always ending with "I love you." "Putting up" with me—frequently too driven—deserves, at minimum, beatification. If sainthood were possible for someone Jewish, I would recommend her. I've never heard her badmouth anyone. She is smarter than I, though minus my go-ahead-and-try chutzpah. Quiet, but deep, she is thinking all the time—sometimes rethinking too much. When she received her master's degree in social work at Barry University a few years ago, she got just one "B"—the rest "A"s. Why that "B"? The professor said she didn't speak up enough in class!

I am enormously proud of our five children—David III, Jennifer, Amanda, John, and Dana—and their families. They are "good people"—I have no higher compliment. How they do, how they feel, is so important to me. I want them to be what they are—people of good values who feel good about themselves, and who make a difference in others' lives. If you want to really please me, say something nice about someone in our family.

Any regrets? I wish that I had given everyone in my family more time. But I do know that I—with my wife, Roberta—did give our children the values that will sustain them all their lives.

To say that how hard I worked did not have a downside for family would be disingenuous. To this day, I've yet to meet anyone who said, "I spent too much time with my family." Nor I. To this day I have worried about the effect on my family of how I spent my waking hours and how often we moved.

On the other hand, our children had more adventures than most children. They did get to visit a number of countries and meet especially interesting people (including the President of the United States), and to be with us at St. Peter's in the Vatican, where our first grandchild was baptized. They grew up in homes where we went to church every Sunday and knelt nightly to say prayers. They never heard Mommy or Daddy ever say things about other people in the privacy of our home that we would not say in public. Their parents never tried drugs, even as the two of us came of age in the hazy early days of a cultural revolution that included marijuana and more. The only times we ever had a drink—perhaps two glasses of wine—would be when hosting a dinner at home or when we went out with others. I am confident all five of our children knew we loved them. My goal was to get home before they went to bed; usually, I did. But I also know that my wife was their saving, ever-present grace—and my own.

Our five children today live in four states and five cities. I speak with each at least once every week, never failing to end a phone call with, "I love you." We're all together—seven grandchildren, too—every Thanksgiving or Christmas. You may hear me say, "I'm only as happy as my unhappiest child." You can usually "fix" things when children are four or even fourteen. But children grow up and have "adult" problems. You are there to help whenever you can. But they are like you— most times, you have to fix it yourself, if you can.

You don't go through life without pain. Loved ones die. My parents. My brother Pelham, full of life in his forties and the president of Perdue Farms, dead without warning from a heart attack. Our son-in-law Jesse lost suddenly, accidentally. Moments of agonizing pain made me stronger; if I can survive such loss, other challenges are put in perspective. It is a reminder, of course, of your own mortality. That you never again will see a loved one in your lifetime is an awesome thought.

You cannot prepare for any of this, but you can pray. I do so every morning, on rosary beads blessed by Pope Francis. The passing of loved ones reminds you of what is truly important in this world—and the next. (I cannot fathom a meaningful life without a sense of Higher Being and Heaven.) I have arrived at a point in life where I am eager to be in a house of worship every week, but not necessarily my own. Frequently, Bobbie and I have been the only white people in a service surrounded by black people. I am usually the one who says on a Friday, "Let's go to Temple Judea." We have been to mosques and taken a course in Islam. We have visited Hindu and Sikh temples. We have been in the constant presence of one God everywhere.

My life has been a juggling act. I've dropped some balls. But now is too late for a do-over. I've made my choices and lived with them.

I won't leave behind much money, but will leave some wisdom. Benjamin Franklin reminds us, in a letter he wrote to his mother: "I would rather have it said, 'He lived usefully' than, 'He died rich.'"

Within this book are the lessons of my life, how I learned them and from whom, and how they might be useful for others.

My life has been full; still is. Nightly, I go to sleep eager for the next day's adventure. My lifelong hunger has been for fairness, for justice, for decency, for love. My mother told me once that I was a "romantic." She meant it as a compliment. I took it that way. Still do.

My story has everything to do with children—with my own childhood, my own children, everyone's children.

INTRODUCTION

CHILDHOOD TO CHILDREN

*"I slept, and dreamt that life was joy. I awoke and saw that life was service.
I acted and, behold, service was joy."*
—Rabindranath Tagore, Bengali thinker and poet

"Authentic power is service."
—Pope Francis

It is a summer morning, hot and humid, headed toward a scorcher. I am at an early learning center in Liberty City, Miami's most challenged neighborhood. Most of the children here live in poverty. Some of these children will grow up to do wonderful things for themselves and others. Some will grow up and hurt themselves, and other people. Some won't grow up at all.

A semicircle of little children embraces me. Twenty-one children—three and four years old—jostle to be as close as they can. The book I am going to read is *Old MacDonald Had a Farm*. In my time, which would be their grandparents' or great-grandparents' time, "Old MacDonald" was more jingle than book, sung to me before I was five years old, and it started this way: *"Old MacDonald had a farm. E-I-E-I-O. And on his farm he had a cow. E-I-E-I-O. With a moo moo here. And a moo moo there. Here a moo, there a moo. Everywhere a moo-moo. Old MacDonald had a farm. E-I-E-I-O."* Verse upon verse calls forth a succession of animal sounds for pigs, ducks, horses, lambs, chickens.

Farmer MacDonald on the cover is dressed in overalls, complete with suspenders and a red-and-white checked shirt. On his head is a straw hat. From that hat emerges two bunny ears.

When I read a book with children, I ask many questions. Mine today begins with the cover. "What kind of animal is this?" I ask. No one knows. Two guess "Cow." No one says "Rabbit."

My grandchildren at that age would have known. Millions of other American children at that age know, too. Yet in a country where four million children are born each year, an astonishing number of three- and four-year-olds—hundreds of thousands—are in pretty much the same place as these twenty-one children.

When these children enter kindergarten, what will be their chances of success? How many students, and lives, will be lost? How many lives will never reach what could have—should have—been?

The children not knowing it was a bunny rabbit was my "aha" moment. For more than two decades now, I have talked with experts, understood the brain science, read book after book. But this one moment with Mr. MacDonald was my wake-up call. The moment when I come to understand that if we lose these children, we have lost more than them—we have lost what they might invent, lead, research, discover, or give. The very future of our country depends on these children—*all* children—having a real chance to succeed. What can I do about this? How did I come to realize this? That is *the* story of my life. It is this story.

To arrive where I am today, I begin three-quarters of a century ago. All the years of my life fit together in one story, though not seamless. Reading is central to every one of those years—central to how I grew up, central to my thirty-five years in journalism, central to my twenty years of work on behalf of the future of children. Children who cannot read are an avoidable tragedy. Mine is all one story in multiple chapters blended throughout in one life of purpose.

~ ~ ~

Age four is the first year I can remember. It was then my mother read to me *The Little Engine That Could.* Seven decades later, I see this very book as a splendid metaphor for a meaningful life: "I think I can. I think I can." That little engine *could*, and *did.*

That book—and my mother—got me off to a great start on reading. We had no kindergarten where I lived; still, because of her, I was reading by age five. First grade began with the "Dick and Jane" series. A few years later, we had all nineteen volumes of the *World Book Encyclopedia* at home, giving me the pleasure of reading each volume for the joy of lifelong discovery. My parents—and teachers—gave me a lifelong love of reading. I still read at least a book every week, sometimes several.

I was given a love of words. My wife Roberta knows even more words than I. Not infrequently, we will awaken at 3 a.m. or so and play word games. Words have been my life and career. Words, used wisely and with civility, lead to meaningful conversation, real communication, and better lives.

I have been able to do more in life by expecting good people and goodness. Anne Frank, writing in her diary while in hiding during the Holocaust, penned these words: "How wonderful it is that nobody need wait a single moment before starting to improve the world." Perhaps naïve, but it works for me, too. Sometimes my trusting being gets me burned. Nonetheless, I remain the "romantic" my mother thought I was. A dreamer, too. "Not much happens without a dream," Robert Greenleaf wrote in his essay "The Servant as Leader," adding, "And for something great to happen, there must be a great dream. Behind every great achievement is a dreamer of great dreams." I am a realist, too. Are there bad people in this world? Yes. Evil people, too. But there are far more good people who want their lives to be meaningful in ways that transcend their lifetimes.

Even in these hyper-partisan times, I feel optimistic that what made this country reach moments of greatness can make our nation even greater. Most Americans share great human values that can lead, with vision and hard work, to lives of meaningful achievement built from purposeful energy.

I have led two very different "careers"—newspapers and early learning—both built from a childhood and life experiences that prepared me for all that would follow.

For me, a single theme will endure to my last breath: the exhilarating joy of service. Service to others, especially to the youngest. That has made my life meaningful. Money never much interested me. Nor did cars or country clubs. I've loved sports, but I've never had the inclination to make the time to play golf or tennis.

My father was a newspaperman in this country's biggest metropolis, New York City; then he became a chicken farmer in the hamlet of Sandy Pond, New York, and next a deeply respected reporter in Florida. I always wanted to exceed his expectations. I still do. I want others to do no less than meet my expectations; the best people will exceed them.

At times I have been labeled obsessive, a workaholic, intense, driven, ambitious. Some labels do fit; others are exaggerated. (I've despised the label "workaholic"; if I love my work, why is that a negative?) I do have a temper at times, but am never purposefully hurtful to anyone. I am willing to apologize when I act "stupid," and I do sometimes act stupidly. I've never had ulcers because frustration is not permitted to feast within me. I am never vengeful.

When something needs to be done, I do it as immediately as possible. Or earlier. I do not "chill out." Vacations are mostly for learning; it is a joy to learn, and grow. I cannot rest until whatever I have to do is accomplished.

I am my parents' son, raised in awareness of a purpose beyond myself and this time on earth. I have lived an impatient life, intent on wasting none of my time as a mortal being. I keep saying "Yes" to most things and to most people—connect someone who needs a job, agree to make a speech somewhere, serve on boards that make a difference in other lives, undertake a major project. Seldom do I say "No." I am not saving my energy for the next world.

An appetite for fairness was my North Star for thirty-five years as reporter, editor, or publisher: Get it right—exactly right and in context. Be as fair and objective as humanly possible. In more recent years, I have applied those same lessons on behalf of children. *Every* child deserves a genuine opportunity to succeed in school and in life. That's only...fair.

Over the years it began to dawn on me that the consequences of many of the stories—so often tragedies—I covered, or edited, had their roots in childhood. The abused and neglected child so often grew up to abuse others. Many of the calamities that make up the news could have been averted if only—*if only*—a childhood had been different. A much loved child, an attentive and nurturing parent, a child who loves to play, a child who early on learns to read—that is most often the child who will grow up to succeed.

Years later, I came to know the words and the wisdom of Lillian Katz, the early childhood advocate and educator:

> We must recognize that the welfare of our children is intimately linked to the welfare of all other people's children. After all, when one of our children needs lifesaving surgery, someone else's child will be responsible. . . . The good life for our own children can be secured only if a good life is secured for all other people's children.

I will come back to all this, but I had better begin at the beginning. My story begins in New York City during the first few months of our country entering World War II, where I began to understand, without quite being aware of it, just how important it is for every girl and boy to have what I had—a much-loved childhood, embedded in lessons and support that would preface, and prepare me for, a good life to be.

CHAPTER 1

EARLY LIFE AND FAMILY

*"Train up a child in the way he should go,
and when he is old, he will not depart from it."*

—Proverbs 22:6

My parents loved each other deeply through more than four decades of marriage. Only death could separate them. Both were sure they would be reunited in Heaven. David and Nancy Lawrence had five children between 1940 and 1945. Being "romantics," they came to think it would be good to raise children on a farm. So they bought thirty-three acres in Sandy Pond, New York, almost fifty miles northwest of Syracuse on the heel of Lake Ontario, three hundred miles and seemingly a thousand years removed from our previous home in New York City. Our telephone number was just four digits—2651.

They knew nothing about farming, but they had read Betty MacDonald's hugely popular 1945 book, *The Egg and I,* a fish-out-of-water tale about a city couple that moves to a chicken farm, faces almost overwhelming (frequently comic) challenges, and finally succeeds—sort of.

My father, a newspaper reporter at the storied *New York Sun* during the Forties, thought he could have a couple of cows, many chickens and not so many turkeys, a few goats, some sheep, one horse (all of which we had)—and do some work for the weekly *Sandy Creek News* and maybe write a book, neither of which he ever did. Farming took up all his time. My mother, among the privileged few in the Social Register (the blueblood bible of that era), found herself plucking chicken feathers. She did so willingly; I cannot remember her ever complaining about anything except old age. Quite ill in the last year of her life, she asked, not expecting an answer: "Do you know how tough it is to grow old?" Our farm needed everyone to make it work. It was there that my siblings and I labored before dawn, before catching the school bus along Rural Free Delivery Route No. 2.

The first five children, of which I was No. 2, were born in New York City—I at my maternal grandparents' home on March 5, 1942. Their apartment building at 270 Park Avenue, more or less kitty-corner from The Waldorf Astoria hotel, was a setting of privilege.

I came to be in a family, especially on my mother's side, that cared about the details of the past. My baby book, penned in my mother's handwriting, tells me that I made my entrance at "4:43¼ a.m." (precision always has been important to the Lawrences), weighing in at eight pounds, eight and a half ounces. "Davey was slightly cold at birth," my mother wrote, "but Dr. Greeley's nurse, Miss Mugford, put a hot water bottle at his feet and he was soon as warm as toast. The doctor and nurse left at about 6:15 a.m." My complexion was described as "very fair"—three-quarters of a century later I have unusually "fair" skin—and my eyes as "deep blue."

This was eighty-eight days after we entered World War II. Our side wasn't yet winning. Franklin Delano Roosevelt was President. We were developing the atomic bomb (though only a relative handful of Americans knew it), which would end the war in August 1945. Though I was too young to recognize it, the war touched everyone's life in America. At my baptism at St. Patrick's Cathedral in New York, my grandfather, Joseph W. Lawrence, stood in as godfather for his son and my father's brother, Robert T. Lawrence, who was at sea aboard the battleship *USS Arkansas*, which was on convoy duty escorting merchant ships across the Atlantic.

My mother and father were New York people. Both came from large, financially successful families, bearing substantial expectations and obligations.

My mother, Nancy Wemple Bissell, born the same year (1917) as the United States entered World War I, came from a socially prominent family. She made her "debut" in the Thirties at a dinner dance at The Waldorf Astoria. Her family, proud of its Mayflower Society membership, traced its American heritage to a genuine Pilgrim, Richard Warren, who arrived aboard the *Mayflower* in 1620. (Through my mother, our family lineage can be traced all the way back to 1057 in Florence, Italy.)

Send away, I did, for a DNA swab, and it revealed that most of my ancestors came from northwestern Europe, primarily Great Britain and Ireland. All humans have traces of Neanderthal DNA, but I have a tad more than most. This will not surprise some of the people who have worked with and for me.

Mother, the middle of seven children, came from a high Episcopal family with a tradition of service and accomplishment. Her father—Pelham St. George Bissell—was President Justice of the Municipal Court of New York City. She never went to college, but she was smart and well-rounded, having traveled with her family to Europe in the late 1920s when few Americans did. A few years later, she fell in love—deeply—with David Lawrence, born the same year she was. They were so much in love that newspaper folks thought it was worth writing about. "Cholly Knickerbocker," the pen name of the best known New York society columnist of his time, wrote these words in the *Journal-American* in the winter of 1938:

> David is Nancy's constant companion these wintry days.... One cannot help but note their devotion to each other. Neither Nancy nor David has any interest in our junior "Café Society." You'll never see them at the Stork Club, and I doubt if they've ever been to the Kit Kat Club— they prefer the more conservative social life.

Or this from another writer in *The New York Times* from 1939: "Never have I known two persons more in love than Nancy and Dave—and it is my 'hunch' theirs is one Mayfair marriage that will 'take.' "

It "took." Married on October 7, 1939, their wedded life of forty-four years was way too short for them, and for their children.

When she married my father, the woman we came to know as "Mommy" converted to Roman Catholicism, making her, of course, more Catholic than many Catholics, for converts often learn more than those of us who grow up and remain in one religion. When we moved to upstate New York, attending Mass at either St. John the Evangelist Catholic Church in Pulaski or St. Frances Cabrini Church in Lacona would be an every-Sunday imperative. We would march in and "own" a whole pew. My father always put two dollars—real money, in those days—in the collection basket.

Through all our growing-up years, everyone in the family knelt for prayers every evening at eight o'clock. Even after all nine children were gone from home, my mother and father still knelt for prayers around 10 p.m.

My mother adored Daddy. He came first. We children were a strong but definite second. Anything he wanted—even moving to a chicken farm—she did not out of obligation, but out of love.

Many people refer to their mothers as "sainted." Mine was. Until Daddy died, we always thought our Irish Roman Catholic father was the strong one in the family. Mommy's two decades of widowhood told us that she might have been even stronger. This tiny (not even five feet tall) woman's strength was buttressed by deep faith and great values. (My eternal optimism and belief in the fundamental goodness of people come from her.)

My father's family heritage is Irish. Members of his extended family came to the United States during the Irish potato famine in the mid-1800s. The Irish of the nineteenth century weren't very welcome in America—the story of so many immigrants—and you had to be tough to survive. Daddy was the youngest of eleven children, a special and perhaps tough place to occupy. A legendary cutup as a child, he surely was "tamed" some by my mother. Daddy grew up mostly on Long Island in a banking family of some success. Some of my

earliest years were lived in Babylon on Long Island's
South Shore.

My father was graduated in 1939 from Manhattan College,
an all-men's college in the Bronx, a Christian Brothers school
founded in 1853. In my father's 1939 college yearbook,
you see a confident young man—perhaps 5 feet, 8 inches—
staring directly into the camera with a knowing half-smile.
The accompanying caption describes a student who spent
much of his time as editor of both the yearbook and the
student newspaper.

During his college summers, he worked at the storied *New
York Herald Tribune*. Upon graduation, he worked briefly at
his hometown newspaper, the *Babylon Leader* on Long Island.
Within months, he had landed a job as a reporter for the *New
York Sun*, a conservative Republican newspaper in a city which
then boasted eight dailies. He covered the black-market meat
scandal and other profiteering scandals during World War II
and made enough of a mark to be favorably mentioned in A. J.
Liebling's classic collection of journalistic stories, *The Press*.

As a political writer in the forties, my father interviewed the
likes of Harry Truman, Thomas Dewey, Fiorello LaGuardia,
and Averell Harriman, and joined the press corps covering
Franklin Delano Roosevelt's 1944 presidential re-election
campaign. I inherited my love of politics and government from
my dad. (*The Sun* was where, in 1897, eight-year-old Virginia
O'Hanlon wrote to the editor, who responded with the famous
editorial: "Yes, Virginia, there is a Santa Claus.")

When he joined *The Sun*, my father adopted the professional
name D. G. Lawrence, even though his birth certificate carried
no middle name. (The "G" stood for George, his Catholic
confirmation name.) This was to differentiate himself from
the already well-known newsman and nationally syndicated
conservative columnist David Lawrence, who had founded the
United States News magazine, later known as *U.S. News & World
Report*. My father wrote under the byline D. G. Lawrence for the
rest of his life.

He would return to newspapering after eight years on the farm, a tale to be told in the next chapter. In 1956, we moved from the bitter cold of upstate New York, and he—and we—had to start all over again. He began by selling real estate—he needed a job, and seemingly anyone could sell homes and land in 1956 go-go Florida.

That lasted just months until he could return to newspapering—first as the real estate reporter and editor, then the general manager and managing editor of the *Sarasota News* (at that time the smallest city in the country with three daily newspapers). He joined the *Orlando Sentinel* in 1966 as a political reporter, moving to Tallahassee as the *Sentinel*'s state capital bureau chief in 1968. He became known as "the voice of Tallahassee," deeply respected for fairness as well as facts.

A longtime cigar and cigarette smoker—tobacco being the plague of newspapermen for generations, including me for two decades—my father was done in by cancer at the age of sixty-six on September 4, 1983. Gov. Bob Graham and members of the state cabinet honored him with prayer and words of tribute. The governor called him "a professional journalist, a valued historian of Florida politics and government, and a personal friend."

"His many accomplishments leave us all with an enriched state and warm memories," the governor told *Orlando Sentinel* writer John Van Gieson, who wrote the newspaper's lengthy Page One obituary. A *Sentinel* editorial said this: "What made his brand of journalism so special was the way he went about it. His idea of digging for a story was not simply to sit patiently in the Capitol press gallery. He knew better than that. He knew the best way he could cover state government was to get to know everyone and anyone in Tallahassee. And he almost did. Because of that, he often knew what was going to happen before it became enshrouded in officialdom. And so did his readers."

My father was inducted into the Florida Newspaper Hall of Fame in 1990. The press gallery that rises over Florida's House of Representatives in the state Capitol bears his name. That I was later inducted into that same Hall of Fame meant much more to me because I would be alongside my father.

I adored my mother and perhaps worshipped my father—and deeply loved and admired both. As my father's first son and namesake, we naturally would have a special bond, but it went beyond that. He remains my role model.

When he was a farmer, I wanted to be a farmer and, hence, intended to attend Cornell University's well-known agricultural school. When he returned to the newspaper business in 1956, there was no doubt in my mind—I would go into journalism.

I grew up in a family where time and energy were not to be wasted. Expectations were clear. For example, coming home with great report cards—in academics and especially deportment—was always expected. I did not always achieve those expectations.

Nine children in our family added up to lots of people to feed, lots of clothes to buy, lots of people to educate. Every one of us was graduated from either the University of Florida or Florida State University. Our "choices" for higher education had to be affordable, meaning either four years at a state university or maybe start with two years at what was then called "junior college." Nobody was talking about Harvard (even if we had been smart enough). We knew what would be "real" for us. Scholarships and work would be absolutely necessary.

Today, the nine Lawrence children have nineteen degrees of higher learning, and every one of us has led a life fulfilling some honorable measure of success.

My mother and father molded us, with love—sometimes tough love—into a family of strivers, a family of givers, people who feel obliged to make a difference in this world. Contemplating less was impermissible.

My sister Annetje would tell it this way: "Most of the family is absolutely driven. If I have a minute to do something, I'll fill that time. That was a family trait. Hey, it could be cleaning a house or fixing cracks in the floor. We will do it and we will do it *right now.*"

I try to remember what each of our parents taught us over the years, and find myself not remembering who said what because they were so inseparable in their values. "Be there for each other," we were told. "Watch out for each other." "Always tell the truth." "You need to care about other people." And: "You are Lawrences, and you are expected to make something of yourselves."

Living up to my parents' expectations, particularly my father's, remains a driving force of my life. When I became publisher of the *Detroit Free Press* in 1985, it meant less to me because my father no longer was alive. Sharing the news with him would have been much of the joy.

Cancer took my mother's life, too. Also a cigarette smoker, she died in 2003. For two decades she missed terribly the man she always called "David." She was a person of the deepest Catholic faith. I never saw her "mournful" because she simply *knew* they would be reunited in Heaven.

All these years later, I miss them every day. My morning always begins with a prayer that includes both of them. Mommy always said: "All I want is your happiness." She gave us much more.

They instilled in us values of purposeful energy and achievement for ourselves and on behalf of others. Reading was a large part of this. I can still see my father, until the end of his life, sitting in *his* chair and reading. Books were a huge part of growing up and the staple of every child's Christmas and birthday.

My mother brought to the marriage, and to her children, the books of her childhood.

Because of her, I read every one of the twenty-eight volumes of Martha Finley's *Elsie Dinsmore* series, written from the perspective of Elsie, age eight, until very full adulthood, beginning with her childhood memories of the nascent Ku

Klux Klan. Published between 1867 and 1905, these books introduced me to a lifelong love for history.

Because of my mother, I also read two dozen of the colonial and Revolutionary War books by Alice Turner Curtis, written from 1913 to 1937. The titles all started in the same way: *A Little Maid of Ticonderoga, A Little Maid of Bunker Hill*, etc. And I read my mother's old copies of *St. Nicholas Magazine* for children, supplemented by my own subscription to *Jack and Jill Magazine*.

My first-grade year was in 1948 at Sandy Creek Central School. That's when I started reading the *Dick and Jane* series. The edition of my first-grade year (which I have) shows a "typical" American family that actually wasn't typical—all white, living in an idyllic postwar suburban house, a friendly police officer always close by, and Father dressed in a vest and tie in the family garage-workshop helping young Dick make a birdhouse.

When I was eleven, my parents splurged for the *World Book Encyclopedia*. It was used for much more than homework. The oldest of us children would thumb through volume after volume, eager to learn things that we didn't even know we wanted to learn. It was fun to learn then. Still is.

Growing up, of course, couldn't be all sweetness and soft light. We were a "normal" family, with good times and bad, and I was a reasonably "normal" child, on good behavior sometimes, less so other times. There were consequences for the latter. Mommy and Daddy came from the "old school" of discipline. "Bad words" meant your mouth would be washed out with soap. Greater infractions meant corporal punishment. Daddy used a doubled-up belt, Mommy a hairbrush. None of it was extensive, but it was real. Mommy cried when she administered punishment; it truly hurt her more than it did us. Though I strongly believe corporal punishment shouldn't be used—there are wiser and better ways to teach a lesson—I bear no scars, physical or psychological.

A much more pleasant memory came during dinnertime. Our parents had style. Dinner was served on a tablecloth and by candlelight. We sat around one large table, enjoying food grown on our own farm and each other—and a nightly challenge. The patriarch would quiz us on politics, government, other current events and, of course, about our school day. Family ridicule would descend upon anyone who couldn't name such basics as the governor. We were, after all, raised to be informed—and competitive.

We must have been the only farming family in that area that received the Sunday *New York Herald Tribune*. We definitely were the only farming family in that area that played croquet—and highly competitive croquet, at that. (I still play croquet with our own children and grandchildren.)

Above all, however, our parents' expectations began with "making something" of ourselves. It was not about money, but rather about living a life that would make a difference in other lives. We were expected to like learning, and be knowledgeable of the larger world, especially about history and politics. We were expected to be fair to everyone and conscious of our blessings. It furnished a whole life of idealism and optimism. That's why I went into journalism. That's why I came to decide that the highest use of my life should be on behalf of children.

My father used to warn me about not trying to "save the world." But he, and my mother, thought I surely should do my part. That is why I do what I do.

Now let me tell you more about that farm, and how it fit into my future...

A Life Lesson Learned:

Growing up in a home of high expectations, we were each encouraged—pushed may be the better word—to be the best we could be. I have expected the same from our children, and from everyone else. Most people do rise to expectations and challenges. Good things get done by good people. The world progresses.

CHAPTER 2
THE FARM

"The Gross Domestic Product measures everything except that which makes life worthwhile."

—Presidential candidate Robert F. Kennedy

Hard work and telling the truth were the minimum required in our family.

I learned that on the farm—mostly a chicken farm. Raising chickens. Slaughtering chickens. Plucking chickens. Selling chickens to the local grocery. Milking cows. Shoveling manure. Planting vegetables. Harvesting them. Selling some; eating the rest.

How did we—a New York City family of some professional and social standing—end up on a farm in remote, rural, way-upstate New York?

We were living at the time with my maternal and widowed Grandmother Bissell in a large, second-floor apartment at 128 Willow Street in Brooklyn, not far from the East River and the Brooklyn Bridge. Our grandmother—I can remember her only in a wheelchair, beset by arthritis—joined us in Brooklyn after my grandfather died, leaving her alone for a while in that cavernous Park Avenue apartment she had shared with her jurist husband.

I remember those years incompletely but fondly. What stands out is playing in the great mass of snow that nearly buried New York City during the Great Blizzard of 1947. My siblings and I flopped backward into the snow, spreading our arms and legs and creating "snow angels."

The war was over and my father was advancing in his newspaper career, but a back-to-the-land movement was attracting many across urban America, some of that inspired by the bestseller, *The Egg and I.*

Five children already had arrived (Mary, me, Annetje, Betsey, and Pelham); four more would follow (Eileen, Antonia, Joe, and Gabrielle). To my parents, life on a farm would be a fresh postwar start, more suitable, more promising, more healthy for the brood. My parents, basically "city people," wanted what my father called "the simple life." We'd raise some animals. Plant some crops. In his "spare time," my father could write The Great American Novel. There turned out to be no "spare time." A real life cannot be "planned."

My parents assembled three thousand dollars and bought a farm in an area called Sandy Pond, about five miles west of the village of Sandy Creek, population 2,500—in way-upstate New York, fifty miles northwest of Syracuse. They bought it from the Strout Realty Catalog, sight unseen. Who but "romantics" would take such a risk?

On my sixth birthday, March 5, 1948, our family of seven took a six-hour car trip to our new home, that farm in upstate New York.

Life was supposed to be an "adventure," as my parents saw it. We children were raised to view change as exciting and full of possibility.

The original farmhouse—red with white trim, a light blue door and a blue shingled roof—could perhaps be called "charming," but absolutely not "modern." My parents spruced up the place, planting tulips, irises, and a lilac bush bearing purple blossoms; they wanted us to see beauty everywhere. Initially, just three bedrooms were available for one set of parents and five children—three girls, two boys—and others to arrive soon. Meals were cooked on a wood-burning stove. A coal furnace furnished the heat. A water pump dominated the kitchen sink. One bathroom inside; one outhouse, soon to be gone. In the years to come, our abode would be enlarged.

Our home was set back from the road, and separated from there by a white fence. A sign in front called our home "Dovecote," bespeaking my parents' eagerness for peace and domesticity—and elegance. A great silver maple dominated the front yard; under it, in warm weather, resided a playpen for the youngest in the growing brood. There was always the expectation that things would, with God's oversight, "work out." They did. We never, ever thought we were poor.

My father and mother had it all worked out. They were partners. They would have a vegetable garden and some animals. A meadow behind our home would furnish hay for the cows. Mommy was on the inside, doing such as "putting up" tomatoes and other vegetables in Ball Mason jars for the winter months. Outside, Daddy was in charge.

Farm work was demanding, frequently exhausting and never-ceasing in any weather. Winter could be brutal. Temperatures plunged to twenty degrees below zero—sometimes much lower. The infamous "lake effect" meant snowstorms would roll in off Lake Ontario. Thirty-six or more inches of snow could fall in twenty-four hours. Snowdrifts came up to the top of our home. Dagger-sharp icicles, up to three feet long, menaced us from roof edges. No matter the weather, chickens still had to be fed and cows still had to be milked. Just to get to the barn could mean digging a path through snow piled several feet high. (White stuff from the sky also meant we could build snow forts and pummel each other with snowballs.)

Everybody had a vital role in the farm—and family— succeeding. Chores don't get done, we don't eat. Real work, we were made to learn, is both hard and noble. We, beginning with my father, had to learn to farm. *The Country Gentleman* magazine helped in that. So did the wisdom of a neighboring farmer, Harwood Lindsay, from whom we purchased the feed for our livestock. Some of our how-to-be-a-real-farmer education was simply try-and-try-again. Some was like riding a bike; once learned, you never forget. (Decades after my farm years, I had the opportunity to milk a cow; I hadn't forgotten.)

As the oldest son, and bearing the name of my father, I was expected not only to do my share but to set an example.

By the time I was ten years old, I was driving a green-and-yellow John Deere tractor and selling vegetables to neighbors. With a cart behind the tractor, I would sell fresh peas, string beans, corn, radishes, carrots, and turnips to nearby summer cottage residents on Sandy Pond. Not a nickel went to me. It was simply my obligation in helping the family. I never expected anything extra beyond my allowance of twenty-five cents a week, enough to build a collection of comic books at five cents each.

Driving a tractor was fun. Not so much fun was this: five days a week, before we were picked up by the school bus on the dirt road in front of our home, we children rose before dawn to help slaughter, gut, and "dress" chickens that, in turn, were sold to area grocery stores.

We raised some chickens for eggs and our own eating, but mostly we bought poultry from neighboring farms that we would then slaughter and ready for sale. My father (the college graduate and former newspaperman) slit the chickens' throats over a trough, so the blood could run down, then dipped the carcasses in scalding water, so as it make it easier for my mother (still on the Social Register) to run the whirling rubber-tipped machine that took off most of the feathers. We older children learned how to remove the remaining pinfeathers and cut the exact spot so the feet would depart—and then clear out the chicken's innards. The youngest children cleaned the gizzards and such. We were all expected to learn fast, and contribute quickly.

Then we went to school.

After school, quite often, I would accompany my father on his chicken-buying rounds. We'd bring chicken crates, and I'd catch those scampering, frenzied, totally uncooperative little devils by the leg with a pole and hook. It was hard, dusty work, and I always came home with scratches. On the way home, the back of the station wagon filled with chickens inside wooden crates, we always stopped for a five-cent chocolate ice cream cone. (It remains my favorite flavor.)

Even now, it is remarkable to think of my mother (Mayflower Society, graduate of the Spence School on the Upper East Side) participating fully and cheerfully in this blood-spattering, feathers-flying enterprise. "She never had a sense of 'too bad for me,' " my sister Mary recalls. Annetje's memory: "Here she is, a debutante plucking chicken feathers, and it was fine with her. She was so in love with our father, she would follow him anywhere."

Is there a better way to grow up than on a farm and surrounded by a large and loving family? In my grown years, I came to think it was akin to the love I saw with John-Boy and his family on "Walton's Mountain," from that television show of the Seventies. I look back and remember both hard work and good times, with enough siblings to play by ourselves a reasonable game of softball.

The youth development group for farm kids like us, 4-H, was big in my life. There I even learned to sew a bit. My most important 4-H project consisted of my two cows—a young bull and a heifer, the first named "Campy" and the second "Duke" for Brooklyn Dodger baseball stars of that time, catcher Roy Campanella and center fielder Duke Snider. I rooted for the Dodgers, mostly because older sister Mary liked the Yankees. (She also liked the cowboy star Roy Rogers; that meant I *had* to be a Gene Autry aficionado.) The Dodgers were classic underdogs, bereft of a World Series title until that magical fall of 1955 when I was thirteen. (To this day I root for underdogs.) Night after night, a radio close to my ear, I went to bed listening to the thrilling exploits of Campy, Duke, Pee Wee Reese, Jackie Robinson, Gil Hodges and the rest of the Dodgers. The walls of my room, shared with my brother Pelham, were thumbtacked with Dodger pictures from the newspapers.

Radio, then, was a part of our lives. Even today, I listen to radio of those years via satellite radio series like *The Great Gildersleeve, Fibber McGee and Molly, Phil Harris and Alice Faye* and, of course, the cowboy shows like *Hopalong Cassidy* and *Wild Bill*

Hickok. What made it work, then and now, is the pictures I draw in my mind—what the cowboy looked like, the quick-draw of his pistol, chasing the bad guys. Imagination.

The coming of television was a major event of our growing-up years. Where we lived was rural and remote, and for this farm kid, and millions of other people, the outside world had arrived. When network TV came in 1948, I recall townspeople standing in front of Sandy Creek's IGA grocery to see the TV playing in the window. It was that big a deal. We were the second family in our neighborhood to get television—in the fall of 1951, in time to see the epic playoff collapse that year of my beloved Dodgers when Ralph Branca served up that infamous home run ball to Bobby Thomson. It came to be called—rightly so—"the shot heard around the world." On our early Motorola set, I can remember *The Lone Ranger*, *The Jack Benny Program*, the fifteen-minute evening news with John Cameron Swayze, and an abundance of old Charlie Chan movies. We grew up with just four TV networks (ABC, CBS, NBC and DuMont. Nobody foresaw today's hundreds of choices and channels.)

On the farm, we eagerly awaited the arrival of magazines— the aforementioned *Country Gentleman*, *Life*, *Reader's Digest*, *Time*, and the *Saturday Evening Post*. The *Watertown Daily Times* came to our home every afternoon. (Mail delivery came twice a day and once on Saturday on RFD #2; stamps were three cents, postcards just a penny.) On Sunday, my father bought two newspapers—the Syracuse paper and the *New York Herald Tribune*.

We lived on a remote farm, but our parents insisted we be aware of the larger world. My earliest political memory is of my parents weeping early one morning in November 1948, when New York's Tom Dewey lost in an upset to President Truman. Three years later when I was nine, I remember vividly President Truman firing General Douglas MacArthur in 1951 over the latter's making decisions that should have been the President's prerogative. "Too big for his britches," my father said of the general with the giant ego.

Within two walking miles from our farm was the sprawling, sandy Lake Ontario beach. Nearby in a small stream, I caught bluegills and sunfish with a slender bamboo pole and fat worms I dug up myself. I'd catch twenty or so of these small fish, gut them at home, and my mother would fry them for dinner.

The holidays—especially Thanksgiving and Christmas—were extra special for us.

For Thanksgiving in the Fifties, we added another leaf to the already long table so all eight children (Gabrielle wasn't yet born) could more comfortably fit with all that extra food on the table. Daddy would sit at the head, of course, with Mommy just to his right. The mahogany sideboard behind Daddy's chair gleamed with the freshly polished silver tea service our parents had received as a wedding present in 1939. The big Revere silver bowl in the center of the damask-laid table overflowed with grapefruit, oranges, bananas, and grapes. On either side flickered white candles, set within etched hurricane lamps atop silver candlesticks. At the other end of the room stood a mahogany china cabinet with its three shelves behind glass doors and a large cabinet below. Here resided the more elaborate glassware and china that would be used for major occasions such as Thanksgiving and Christmas.

The dining room was papered in subtle silvery blue stripes. A large many-paned window looked out onto the summertime garden and the old apple orchard beyond. A smaller window looked out onto the back field where Daddy had contracted with the owner of a small earthmover to build a small pond for us. My memories of that room also embrace two nineteenth-century oils—one of cows grazing, the other of a girl on a horse—that had belonged to my mother's parents (Mary Valentine Yale Bissell and Pelham St. George Bissell) that hung over the sideboard. Our house had a number of antique chairs and that sideboard, gifts from both the Bissell and Lawrence families.

Every year we enjoyed the same sumptuous Thanksgiving dinner prepared almost solely by Mommy while Daddy took care of farm chores. In addition to the golden brown turkey with the delicious bread stuffing, accompanied by the perfectly browned giblet gravy and the cranberry sauce made with whole cranberries, there were also candied sweet potatoes, creamed onions and peas, assorted dishes of pickles, celery, carrots and radishes, plus the appetizers of grapefruit halves sprinkled with sugar and topped with a maraschino cherry for the children, and shrimp cocktail for the adults. Instead of our usual glass of milk, we'd drink cider while our parents had sherry and maybe some white wine. The dinner was topped off by pumpkin and mince pies with the added richness of hard sauce.

After washing the dishes (a big task in those pre-dishwasher days), we all trooped upstairs for a mandatory nap. Later, we'd finish the day with turkey sandwiches.

Those were cozy Thanksgivings. We had our family about us, and all seemed right about the world.

A month later came Christmas. We were a family eager to believe in Santa, and did—probably long after many other children. Finding out otherwise wasn't easy.

Christmas Eve—right before prayers, and just before bedtime— we hung up our stockings from the mantelpiece above the fireplace. That fireplace danced with flames emerging from crackling wood. Outside, in my memory, it was cold and crisp with a moon so full of light it was magical against the snow.

One year we were all sitting on the rug in front of the fire. Bedtime was a half-hour away, and Daddy told us not to go the woodshed, which was just off the kitchen. It was my older sister Mary, or I, who asked why. Then we both laughed. One of us said, "Of course, we know why, Daddy. All the presents are out there, aren't they?" His response was quick, and stern: "Come on, kids; they are not. Quiet down. You're going to ruin it for the little ones."

"No, the real reason we don't want you going out there," said Mommy, "is that it's too cold. You'll get sick."

After hanging up our stockings, we trooped upstairs to bed—Pelham and me in the closest bedroom, Mary in the middle one, and Annetje and Betsey in the end one, down a miniscule hallway and three steps from Mary's. In fact, it was right over the woodshed, where the presents might be hidden.

Annetje can remember looking out the window at the moonlit snow-covered yard—then up at the sky where in years past she had imagined she saw Santa with his reindeer pulling the toy-laden sled. This night she recalls silently pleading, "Oh, Santa Claus, please, please be real."

At least a couple years I tried to stay awake all night so I could see Santa Claus arrive. I never made it. (One Christmas, brother Pelham convinced me that he had seen Santa. Maybe he did.) I really, really wanted a Red Ryder BB gun, but I never got it. ("You'll shoot your eye out," my mother told me in the same growing-up era depicted in *The Christmas Story* movie that uses those same five words.) But I did get books—among them Robert Louis Stevenson's *Treasure Island* and John R. Tunis' sports sagas—and the deepest pleasure of being able to savor a story that very Christmas afternoon.

If this sounds too good to be true, well, that's how we remember it.

Then, inevitably, life intervened. Setbacks began to pile up for our family. For one thing, a recession struck the nation in mid-1953, lingering for nearly a year and placing additional economic pressure on us. The chicken market wasn't doing well. Money had never been abundant anyway. I can recall enjoying sandwiches of just white bread with either lettuce, or sugar and butter, within. (Growing up with eight brothers and sisters, I learned you eat everything on your plate. Unfortunately, to this day, I still eat everything on my plate. In today's large-portion lifestyle, that is not a good thing.)

Most significantly, my mother became seriously ill. During the early 1950s, she contracted hepatitis; how, I do not know. Winters were especially hard on her. Both my parents did all they could to insulate their offspring from worrying, so we never knew much about any of this.

By the winter of 1955–56, all of this was beginning to be too much, especially on my mother's health.

One frigid evening in January 1956, when I was almost fourteen, we were watching *Arthur Godfrey's Talent Scouts*, televised in the winter months from the Kenilworth Hotel on Miami Beach. My father, seemingly without prior thought, said words like these: "I know what. Children, look up Florida in the encyclopedia. While you're at it, look up New Mexico and Arizona, too." One thing connected all three places—they were warm.

My mother still was recovering from hepatitis. She also had Raynaud's Syndrome, in which a patient's extremities cannot maintain proper body temperature and circulation, leaving a feeling of numbness and cold. The doctor made it clear: Northern New York winters risked her very life. Find a warmer place to live.

The next thing we knew, the farm was for sale, and we were going to move, though we would be in Florida quite a while before our parents ever saw any money. Eventually, they received just six thousand dollars for thirty-three acres, including a home (extensively renovated) and a barn they built, plus that pond. They took a financial bath.

We children didn't know that, and had no idea whatsoever of the risk they were taking in packing us all up to go—not a paycheck coming in—to a strange state.

But we brought with us a lesson that would stand us in good stead all our lives: Be willing to take a risk. Decades later, I would give up major league pay to work on children's issues. Sister Mary would leave her doctorate and big university position to go, at age fifty-eight, to law school. Nobody in our family was hungry for money; everyone thought there were things more important. Our parents gave us that wisdom.

At this very moment back in 1956, we Lawrence children were only focused on the "grand adventure" to come! Alligators! Palm trees! Endless summer! So there we were—two adults, eight children (sister Gabrielle to be born the following year) plus our aristocratic Irish Setter, Sherry, piled into our no-seat-belts, blue-and-white two-door Ford station wagon in the dead of winter that March, bound for Florida, bound for a new life, bound to each other.

A Life Lesson Learned:

Be willing to take risks. My parents surely did. My sister Mary gave up a major league career in university administration to go to law school—at age fifty-eight. I took pay cuts twice, one of them huge. I left thirty-five years of journalism to do something quite different—compensated not in cash, but in more meaningful ways. Not one of us nine children ever thought money was a central dynamic of our lives. Take risks—calculated but real.

CHAPTER 3
FLORIDA AND ADOLESCENCE

*"If a nation expects to be ignorant and free,
in a state of civilization, it expects what never was and never will be."*
–President Thomas Jefferson

We had 1,335 miles to travel to life's next chapter. The day we left Sandy Pond, in March 1956, the thermometer read minus 26 degrees. The next thing I remember is stopping in the North Florida town of Starke in 70-degree sunshine and being treated to glasses of orange juice. There I first saw palm trees. Scraggly ones.

The wars—World War II and the Korean Conflict—were over. The U.S. economy was thriving. Florida—population four million, a fifth of what it is now—was booming. Florida's smallest and most rural counties had most of the political power, but court decisions soon would change that. My father and mother, Republicans all their lives, registered as Democrats, the party with all the power then. That would change. We arrived in a segregated world. That, too, would change.

Our new home would be in the Land of Opportunity. That—and warm weather for my mother—is exactly what we needed. Hard work could take care of the rest.

My parents had decided to make our new lives on Florida's west coast, bordered by the Gulf of Mexico. My father rented a home in the town of Madeira Beach, near St. Petersburg, where we stayed for a month while he searched for a permanent home and a job.

We came to settle thirty-five miles south, in Oneco—once more living aside a dirt road, and walking distance from the town's two stoplights, a grocery store called Barney's, two gas stations, one really big cemetery, a drugstore with a soda fountain and Cokes for a nickel, and an elementary school. Summers were hot, and we never had air conditioning in any of our growing-up years.

Our family lived in an unincorporated town—five miles below Bradenton, eight miles above Sarasota—where, it was said, black folks could not be on the streets after sundown. The time is 1956, two years after the U.S. Supreme Court decided in *Brown v. Board of Education* that "separate but equal" was not equal at all, and therefore mandated school desegregation "with all deliberate speed." Where I lived, and throughout the South, there was no "speed" at all. Some southern governors—Orval Faubus of Arkansas and George Wallace of Alabama, for two examples—mightily resisted all change. Others, like LeRoy Collins of Florida, came to believe in, and work for, racial justice.

Back then, white kids went to Manatee County High in Bradenton (to be renamed just "Manatee High" before my graduation); black kids went to Lincoln Memorial High across the river. Water fountains in grocery stores were labeled "colored" and "white." Black folks could only sit in the balcony in movie theaters. When I was a senior in high school, the sheriff of my county—and sheriffs were very powerful in the South—led the Ku Klux Klan through the streets of black East Bradenton. My senior year class motto was: "We're the best. We're from Dixie. We're the class of 1960."

Coming from the North, I was frequently called a "Yankee." It was not said with affection. Partly, no doubt, it was expressed because I was "the new kid" in town. Far worse, I remember being called a "n----- lover" because even then I spoke up when I heard hate. Those ugly words were tossed around with gratuitous stupidity by a few, though certainly not by most. In our family, as in so many families North *and* South, we were taught that everyone deserved respect. Everyone is God's child. You treat everyone fairly. You treat everyone with decency. No exceptions. Even in my teenage years, I had enough spunk to speak up when I witnessed intolerance, in its raw form or disguised as a so-called "joke." Even then I knew that it should never be "funny" to be hurtful, and that what I say in "private" shouldn't be significantly different from what I would say in "public."

All this furnished memories and lessons for a lifetime of hunger for justice and fairness. As the years have gone by, I have only become more sure of the lessons I learned from my parents and others. For a quarter-century now, the putdown of "politically correct," meaning certain things *cannot* be said even if true, has been prevalent. In fact, I can say anything I want, but am morally obliged—as we all are—to be sensitive as well as truthful.

Newspapering as a career of justice—righting wrongs—came to be my dream. There were lessons to be learned everywhere. In high school I became co-editor of the school newspaper, the *Macohi*. Our remarkable journalism adviser was a woman named Joe Berta Bullock. Just fifty-one inches tall, with braces on both legs, she could walk only with the aid of crutches (though she could drive a car with levers that worked the gas and brake pedals). Her spina bifida meant she could never grow tall and straight.

World War II and its horrors were in the quite recent past. Yet, not yet fifteen years after the war, unthinking teenagers would ink on their wrists or arms the swastika symbol of Nazi Germany. I don't know that any actually understood the evil behind that symbol. (I cannot remember any Jewish students at the school.) The pen-and-ink swastikas at best represented unthinking stupidity.

One day, not thinking that it would end up anywhere, not really thinking at all, a classmate doodled a swastika on an advertisement that was set to go into our paper. The school paper was printed by a process called "offset"; thus, something written on a "flat" containing a pasted story or advertisement could wind up in print. That casual abomination did.

The day that issue of the paper appeared, we were in journalism class, sitting on benches at long tables. Miss Bullock entered the classroom in absolute fury. She took one of those crutches, lifted it over her head and slammed it down on a table.

"My God," she yelled. "Do you know what you have done? Do you know how many people died because of that symbol?"

There are consequences for all that we do. I can never forget that story.

What different times those were.

At the time I was a senior in high school—class of 1960—black and white people were legally forbidden from marrying each other in Florida and twenty-three other states. The word "gay" described happy, joyous people.

Few Americans had ever heard of Vietnam, where 58,000 of their fellow Americans later were to die. (Some of my classmates served in Vietnam. One of my closest friends, a West Point graduate named Bill Rennagel, was grievously wounded in Vietnam in the service of our country.) Haiti was ruled by a despot named Duvalier; Cuba was ruled by the callous Castro, a revolutionary and a dictator who would play a role, indirectly and directly, in my career as a newspaperman.

I had never seen a color TV, except maybe in a *Life* magazine ad. The top TV show was *Gunsmoke*. Top songs included Brenda Lee's "I'm Sorry," Ray Charles' "What I'd Say," the Everly Brothers' "Cathy's Clown," Johnny Mathis' "Misty," and Elvis Presley's "It's Now or Never." You could buy a new car for less than two thousand dollars. (My first car, an eleven-year-old stick-shift 1950 Plymouth Coupe, cost $125; the only "air" came from roll-down windows and a hole in the floorboard on the driver's side.) A gallon of gasoline cost twenty-five cents.

The most recent presidential assassination had been fifty-nine years before, in 1901. Nobody had been to the moon; President John Fitzgerald Kennedy, the man who inspired America to go to the moon, would be assassinated in 1963. There was no internet, no text messages, no Facebook, no Twitter.

I lived, so obvious in retrospect, in a "white world," mostly unaware in many ways of different people and their lives and their challenges. A person of our family's skin color could buy a really special home for no more than fifteen thousand dollars in a nice neighborhood; a black family could not.

In the world in which I lived, I can remember only one young woman in our high school getting pregnant. Such a scandal. (The year we moved south was also the year of *Peyton Place*, the steamy bestseller by Grace Metalious about small-town secrets and sex.) The young woman from my high school, in the practice of those times, was hustled off to a Florence Crittenton Home for mothers-to-be. (Today forty percent of the births in this country are to unmarried women; half of those have no "significant other" whatsoever.)

Just a relative few of us in my graduating class of 373 went from high school to college. (When I was in high school, the Florida of that era had only three state universities—the University of Florida and Florida State, both with only white undergraduates, and Florida A&M with only black students. Today twelve state universities compete for all students. Nationally back then, only 5 percent of the people in law and medical schools were women. Now it is 50 percent or more.) Back then, a graduate of Manatee High could quickly get a job digging a well or a ditch, or selling or fixing cars, or in retail of one sort or another. Nobody was worried about the economic might of China or India or anyplace else competing with us as an economy or in education.

We took for granted that we were the best in the world in education (and we were), and quite sure that we always would be (and we are not). Everyone seemed to be able to get a job; you just needed the bare basics of education. That isn't true now, and never will be again.

When we arrived in Florida in 1956, my father's first priority was to get us settled and back into school. Right behind that, he had to find work.

His first job was selling real estate in a suburban development. In those boom-time postwar days, seemingly anyone could sell anything in the way of Florida land and homes—sometimes, scandalously so, underwater. Houses went up lickety-split. We needed to pitch in to help my father make sure houses were ready for sale. My siblings and I scraped paint and stickers off the windows of newly built and ready-to-sell houses. But sales would be only a stopgap measure for my father. A return to newspapering beckoned.

In that same year of 1956, my father went to work at the *Sarasota News*, first as reporter and editor covering real estate, but quickly rising to manage the whole place. The owner was the wealthy Kent Schuyler McKinley who had started the every-day-but-Sunday newspaper in 1954 with the stated ambition of building a two-party system in Florida and promoting "states' rights." McKinley was a major figure in Florida's transition to Republican power. He was elected to the state legislature, and Sarasota became Florida's first county in the twentieth century to have more Republicans registered than Democrats. Florida, like the rest of the South since the end of Reconstruction, had been a state where Democrats had all the power; that would change before the century closed.

In 1957, the summer I was fifteen, I was making twenty dollars a week in the composing room of the paper my father was running. I learned how to clear big typesetting Intertype machines of hot-lead overflows, known as "squirts," and set headlines by hand. I worked alongside grizzled, tough-talking back-shop veterans with a penchant for gambling. One such game, in which I participated, was called "Traveling." Maybe a dozen of us would spend a nickel on a Coke from the back-shop vending machine. We'd each put up a dollar. On the bottom of every green Coke bottle was etched the place where the soda had been bottled. The one with the city farthest from Sarasota collected from everyone else.

Seldom a winner, I wish I had learned my lesson about gambling right then and there. I did learn, however, not to wager more than I could afford to lose. (For years of post-college newspapering, mostly following late-night shifts, I played five- and seven-card stud, and draw poker, losing as often as I won. But there was one glorious moment, early in my newspaper career when I was dispatched to help cover reapportionment in the state capital of Tallahassee. Accompanied by Martin Waldron, a legendary reporter with an extra and impressive dimension of what seemed to me like real skill in betting, we went to the greyhound racetrack at nearby Monticello.... Three hours later, I returned to the motel and my wife and two-year-old David III. Exuberantly, dramatically, I dumped $180 on the bed. That paid for our first washing machine.)

It was the *Sarasota News*, beginning in 1957, that furnished my first real lessons in journalism. In mid-afternoon, my shift was finished, and the paper was off the press and on the way to newspaper carriers for home delivery. I would need to wait several hours for a ride home with my father. That gave me time to go into the newsroom and beg the city editor for press releases that I could rewrite well enough to put in the paper. Gnarled newspaper editors (decades older than I) would take what I turned in, grumpily insist that it could be much better, and make me try again. What I learned was the most basic secret of good writing: practice-practice-practice.

Newsrooms then remained reminiscent of *Front Page*, that 1931 movie classic of hard-charging, hard-bitten veterans who would do anything to get a good story, and always had a bottle of whiskey in the desk drawer. The chase for a good story made almost everything seem worthwhile. College wasn't necessary in most newsrooms; "journalism school" was often seen as not for "real newspapermen." The reporters and editors were almost always men—except in the "women's section." On-the-job experience often began as a "copyboy," a junior role, to be sure.

Back then, a reporter would finish writing his story, rip it from the typewriter, then bellow, "Copy!" A "kid"—just as likely to be an adult as a teenager—would hustle to bring that copy to the editor. Newsroom pay was mediocre for everyone, including for the people in charge. But the cliché was true then, and always would be for me: You're not in this for the money. You're doing this for the experience, for the training, for the opportunity. I never put in for overtime when I went into full-time journalism; had I done so, "management" would not have welcomed it. The best people, then as now, entered journalism as idealists. They knew they were being paid for being skeptical but not cynical; the best people never strayed into cynicism. Meanwhile, the compensation slowly came to be respectable.

The best journalism is a genuine craft. You never get good enough, but you can get closer. It is art. Not science. You paid your dues with stories and assignments that lacked glamor—writing obituaries, for instance. Then, maybe, you'd get a chance to dig into something, and make the most of it.

(My first byline appeared under a two-column headline on the "Local" front of the *St. Petersburg Times* in the summer of 1960 after my graduation from high school. Age eighteen, I was an intern in that newspaper's Bradenton Bureau. The story? A bumper tomato crop in nearby Palmetto, Florida. It certainly wouldn't be entered in the Pulitzer competition. But it was a big deal for me; you never forget that first byline.)

The more you know, the more you can learn, the better prepared you are for journalism. My father insisted on his three sons going to college, but thought college was "optional" for my sisters; all six sisters thought otherwise. All nine of us would graduate from college.

I was graduated from high school in June 1960, having invited the two leading presidential candidates—John F. Kennedy and Richard M. Nixon—to my graduation. Neither came, but Mr. Nixon did send a letter of congratulations, while Mr. Kennedy sent an autographed copy of his Pulitzer Prize-winning book, *Profiles in Courage*. (I still have both.)

It never hurts to ask; it never hurts to try.

With hindsight, I'd like to say I was all for Senator Kennedy. In fact, though, I was all for Vice President Nixon for reasons I cannot remember and make no sense to me now. In any event, at age eighteen I couldn't vote. You had to be twenty-one then, which didn't change until 1971 and the 26th Amendment to the U.S. Constitution. My first presidential vote came in 1964 when I was twenty-two; Lyndon Johnson over Barry Goldwater was the easy choice for me. Today Johnson is most remembered for the debacle of Vietnam, but also deserves to be known for doing more to advance education and civil rights than any twentieth-century President.

In my first eighteen years I learned the values that have meant everything in my life since, and vitally to my work with children. Now, it was time to go away to school, and learn some more—from books, professors, other students, and in other ways...

A Life Lesson Learned:

Have the courage to speak up. Don't appear to accept by your silence what is unacceptable. What you are willing to say to the world should not be different from what you would say to anyone. There are plenty of things to laugh about, without resorting to so-called "humor" that belittles others.

CHAPTER 4
COLLEGE, COURAGE, AND BOBBIE

"Cowardice asks the question—is it safe? Expediency asks the question—is it politic? Vanity asks the question—is it popular? But conscience asks the question—is it right?"
–Dr. Martin Luther King Jr.

Going to college, in September 1960, would mean for me the University of Florida, 175 miles away.

Even attending low-cost state schools, we Lawrences had to figure out how to pay for it. A whole school year—tuition, books, housing, everything—could be fifteen hundred dollars, a lot of money for us then. Summers, I earned money— forty dollars weekly to start—as a reporting intern at the *St. Petersburg Times*, known for giving young journalists every opportunity to succeed. Working there led to scholarships sponsored by the newspaper and by its owner, the legendarily supportive Nelson Poynter. Then, too, I had a scholarship from the Colonial Dames of America (an essay plus proof of my lineage in this country back to the 1600s), and a winning essay and a hundred-dollar prize from the United Daughters of the Confederacy (though memory cannot recall what made me eligible for that; I had no Southern heritage). My freshman year I also worked nights peddling pastries and sodas in a dormitory café.

My siblings all had similar stories of working one's way through college.

Though journalism would be my future, I started out in political science—a liberal arts education being a great foundation. Later I switched to journalism mostly because it was easier, and I didn't have much time when I became the managing editor and, later, the editor of the *Florida Alligator*, the student newspaper. (In hindsight, I wish I had majored in history.)

In my junior year, in the fall of 1962, UF's undergraduate divisions were desegregated. Half the campus seemed to think it was a reasonable idea. The other half was quite sure that Satan had taken over.

I remember the hatefulness of those students and townspeople who fought integration. What they chanted as others marched for civil rights offended my sense of fairness and justice. (Growing up in upstate New York I can remember just one black family. I didn't know many black people in that state or Florida either. My first black classmate came when I went to the Harvard Business School's Advanced Management Program in the early Eighties.)

What upset me more than a half-century ago—still does—had to do not only with race, but also about anything that didn't seem just. Being fair— justice—is the filter of my life.

The University of Florida then was a quarter of the size it is today, and under assault from the forces of the sanctimonious right, most notably by the Florida Legislature's Johns Committee. From 1956 to 1965, that reactionary McCarthyite force conducted witch-hunting offensives against Florida's state universities, quite sure that all sorts of "Reds" (Communists), homosexuals, anarchists, and other perceived anti-American deviants could be found among professors and students and would need to be rooted out. Civil liberties were assaulted. Some under siege committed suicide. Crazy as it sounds now, it was then quite real.

In that atmosphere, university leaders—dependent on the Legislature's political predilections and funding—wished to shoo away dissent of any sort. That would come to mean some trouble for me.

In my earliest days and months at the University of Florida, I worked hard to get off to a good start on grades. I didn't wander into the student newspaper until after the Christmas break of my freshman year. It changed my life in a way more significant than even journalism could.

Then and there is where I met Roberta Phyllis Fleischman, called "Bobbie" since childhood (though I've always preferred "Roberta"). Her father had died of a heart attack when she was six, and her sister Ellen was four. Her mother came to think Bobbie had rheumatic fever and would benefit from the year-round warmth of South Florida, leading to a move from Queens, New York, to Coral Gables. (Bobbie's not sure she ever was really ill.) At the University of Florida, we both worked as *Alligator* reporters. We were nineteen then. I fell in love instantly, *knowing* she was *the* person for me. Beautiful. Smart. Deep. A really good person.

Our first date was to a Delta Upsilon fraternity party. It went well. Neither of us dated anyone else ever again. (We still laugh over a classmate named Pat Tunstall who told Bobbie that I looked like a "Greek god." She apparently had not seen Zeus or Apollo.)

Comes the spring of 1962, and I have just turned twenty. I'm on a home visit to my scary-size Roman Catholic family. I am standing in the kitchen announcing to my mother that I was in love and "going to marry Roberta Fleischman." My mother, the very soul of naïveté, says, "The name sounds German." To which, my ever-alert sister Annetje immediately responds: "I think it's Jewish."

The only Jewish person in the family I knew was my Uncle Joe—Joseph Schwartz, a lawyer from New York and married to one of my mother's sisters. After I announced my impending marriage, I can remember my father, the traditional Irish Catholic who went to Mass most mornings of his adult life, announcing to all of us in the kitchen: "No one will ever say anything bad about Jews in this home."

My mother would have loved her future daughter-in-law to convert to Catholicism, as she herself had. In March of 1963, nine months before we were to be married, she wrote a three-page letter beginning this way:

> Dear Bobbie. All of us were so happy to meet you. Be assured that you have all of our love!" On the next page, she wrote: "I don't know whether you know it or not, but I was not a Catholic when I met Mr. Lawrence but subsequently became one. I have never regretted it.... Would you (let David) introduce you to the chaplain at Gainesville and take a course of instruction there? Years ago I did this—out of mostly pure love for Mr. Lawrence, and frankly, too, figured if I had to promise to bring my children up in the Catholic faith (a requirement then to be married in the church), I'd better see to it that it was the right one. Whatever way you decide on the above is purely up to you, and I promise no hard feelings on my part or Mr. Lawrence's. I have several (in my family married to non-Catholics), and they are good marriages. But mine has been, and is, such a perfect one that I want the same for you and Davey.

My wife-to-be wrote back a dozen days later:

> I can understand your wish for me to take Catholic instruction—for David's and my sake and for that of our children. Also, I have a natural interest in something that will affect my life to such a great extent. I have planned for some time to attend these sessions, but frankly have been half-afraid that you and Mr. Lawrence would feel hurt if, after contemplating them, I did not become Catholic. Basically, there aren't too many areas where Dave's and my ideas conflict. Because of this, added to what I know of Dave (and his family) and what I have seen of the Catholic Church, I have no real qualms about bringing up our children as Catholics. However, while I am not an extremely religious person, my life, the traditions, beliefs and ways of worship are part of me—and I could never honestly change that. I realize that our lives might be 'smoother'—superficially—if I did

change, but I care too much about my family and yours, and our (forthcoming) family to pretend to be what I am not. The Catholic religion is a warm and beautiful one, and I respect it and want my children to love it—but it is not mine. Dave understands, and I believe we will be wise enough parents that our children will understand.

What an exchange. Roberta Phyllis Fleischman Lawrence was then, is now, quite remarkable and with the greatest decency.

Some days later, my mother responded:

Thank you so much for your lovely letter. Mr. Lawrence and I admire your frankness! I certainly did not intend you to understand that we wanted you to become a superficial Catholic. That would be living hypocrite-style, a quality that is not to be admired.... This is a free country, thank God, and it is entirely up to you.... The subject on our part is now forever closed unless you desire to bring it up again yourself.

My mother, too, was a remarkable person of the greatest integrity.

So, too, my father. He could be tough, erupting occasionally in full Irish temper (as I sometimes do myself). But he and my mother always supported us. And I was fortunate that he never pushed hard on grades in college because grades, except for my first semester, never were much of a priority for me. . . . Back in the Thirties, at Manhattan College he had an abundance of "gentleman's Cs." If those were good enough for him, they would be good enough for me.

I took him at his gentlemanly word.

In college my "A" grades were sparse, "B"s not abundant, and I had my full share of "gentleman's Cs." Along the way, I flunked one course and almost another.

The first was photojournalism under famed professor Buddy Davis, who would go on to receive a Pulitzer Prize in 1971 for his *Gainesville Sun* editorials regarding the desegregation of local public schools. The camera scared me; I wasn't comfortable with it and, especially, with work in the darkroom.

Professor Davis told me he was doing me "a favor" by flunking me (exactly the sort of thing my mother might have said before punishing me). He was right. (No doubt my mother was, too.) I was forced to take another course in photography from Jerry Uelsmann, whose black-and-white photographs and photomontage magic are prized today. This time I did well. The camera became my friend. My "eye" was much improved.

At the tail end of my college years—I graduated in three and a half years—I came *t-h-i-s* close to failing another course. This time the matter of grades was even more serious. But let me work up to this tale:

In the fall of 1963, my last semester of college, I was even busier than my usual running-around self—"multitasking" years before anyone was using the word.

The *Alligator* had moved to publishing five days a week. (With my editorship came a "salary" of thirty dollars a month; it all helped.) I was active in Delta Upsilon. I also was semi-hooked on playing pool for money—mostly 8- and 9-ball. The scene was in the then-Florida Union building, the home of the *Alligator* and, down the hall, a place to play pool and billiards. Betting was forbidden, but I won often enough to think it worthwhile to take that chance. Oh, yes, I did attend some classes.

In early November, a month and a half away from graduation and marriage, I was part of a UF student delegation to the national convention of Sigma Delta Chi (SDX), the national journalism honor society. The setting was Norfolk, Virginia, the then rough-and-tumble Navy town. Seventy college students interviewed chemist and Nobel Prize recipient Dr. Glenn Seaborg, then the well-known chair of the Atomic Energy Commission. Each of us wrote, on-deadline, about that interview. I won first prize—my first national honor. The later-to-be legendary newsman Walter Cronkite presented the check that evening—for fifty dollars. I was on top of the world—for maybe two hours.

Feeling good about myself—and surely full of myself—I agreed to go on the town that evening for "some fun." Believe me—please—I wasn't sure what "fun" would mean, but I went along. "Going along" was stupid. I had to learn the hard way.

Five of us college students went to a home in a neighborhood we didn't know, accompanied by two much older men with whom we never should have been. One of those men knocked on the door. Suddenly, police were rushing the house. (I have since assumed that the police were staking out what they thought was a house of ill repute, but I never did know for sure.) We were being told to put both hands atop a police car, and were patted down before our ride in a police van to the city jail. We were all scared. We stayed awake all night in a dark and dank cell, a few feet away from much older and scary-looking men.

The next morning, an attorney for the local newspaper accompanied us to court, urging us to plead "no contest" to disorderly conduct. We did. The fine was twenty-four dollars apiece. From the check Mr. Cronkite gave me the evening before, I paid my own fine, and another student's—and was left with just two dollars and riches of embarrassment. (My parents said to tell the truth—always—so I called my wife-to-be. I cannot remember her reaction, but I do know that we were married the next month. Ever since, every job application I've ever filled out required my saying whether I ever had been convicted of anything but a routine traffic violation; I've always fessed up.)

My miserable month did not get better. The administration-dominated Board of Student Publications was increasingly weary of me. They, and the university president, saw me as a journalistic "rabble-rouser," and were especially horrified that I would consider—in those tumultuous times—a weekly column from the state NAACP. Less seriously, but no less seriously for them, there was also a "letter to the editor" in the *Alligator* advocating "free love." It wasn't my letter, and—honestly—I am not sure that I knew then what the term meant. But that letter did run, and on my watch. That did not please the powerful people in Tigert Hall, where the administration resided.

Then came Friday, November 22, 1963, thirty days before my graduation day. On the front page of the *Alligator* that morning was an editorial—written by me—suggesting that the selection of my successor as editor was "political" on a campus where student politicians were powerful. That was the last straw for the administration. I was summoned to appear the following Monday before the Board of Student Publications. My goose was surely cooked.

That very afternoon came the United Press International teletype machine four-bell alarm with a "Flash": President Kennedy had been assassinated in Dallas. It was earthshaking. Americans before my time remembered Pearl Harbor—December 7, 1941—as the momentous event of their lifetimes. But in my time—almost four decades before 9/11—it was the assassination of a young, charismatic President.

We put out an "Extra" that day—a model of on-deadline teamwork at a time of national sorrow. I told the Board of Student Publications that I wouldn't show up Monday because it was the day of JFK's funeral. The board members didn't need me there to fire me. And they did.

(Eventually, enough *Alligator* editors were in trouble or dismissed—by an administration-dominated oversight board—that the university came to decide it really didn't need the headache of "freedom of the press." That's how *The Independent Florida Alligator* came to be—off campus. I still love my university and the *Alligator*. Indeed, when my newspaperman father died in 1983, our family honored his memory at UF with a scholarship fund for aspiring political journalists. It's worth noting that I am the only fired *Alligator* editor with an honorary doctorate from the university! Redemption...of sorts.)

What a month: I had won a national award, been arrested, produced an "Extra" on the assassination of JFK, been fired—and still had one big event to go: marriage in Coral Gables at the Church of the Little Flower on December 21, 1963, the same day I was supposed to graduate.

But graduation wasn't a given.

I only remember one course I took that last semester. Why I took it, I do not remember. I never understood what "urban sociology" was—and still really don't know (though I've had it explained to me on several occasions). (Geometry in tenth grade never made any sense to me either, and I've never used it for anything, though I do know what a triangle is! And my college grade in Economics—something that has never made much sense to me—was a D.) I skipped those Urban Sociology classes more times than I attended. It was in no way mature of me to do so. Sooner or later, the bill for this behavior would arrive.

Before I departed Gainesville for Coral Gables, in these pre-email and internet days, I left a self-addressed postcard with the professor so he could send me the grade. Then came marriage. Roberta was so beautiful. We had maybe three dozen people at our wedding, and that included my eight siblings and our parents. The next day, we were on our way to Nassau, five decks down on a ship called the *Bahama Star*, built in 1931, a troop carrier in World War II. No way did it resemble a sleek twenty-first century cruise ship.

I was nervous all through the honeymoon. Part of that is natural for newlyweds. But there was another reason. My first day of work at the *St. Petersburg Times* was to be the next to last day of December 1963, a Monday. We arrived back in Miami two days before, with my anxiety heightened. If I didn't pass that one class, I wouldn't graduate. Pass, and I had my degree and was cleared to go in comfort to my first real job. Fail, and... who knows?

Awaiting me was the postcard and the grade I dreaded from Urban Sociology. "D--," the professor wrote. That's a D with two (!) minuses. "I am only giving you this because I think you will amount to something," he added.

That remained to be seen. The newlyweds headed off to St. Petersburg, one of them a barely legitimate college graduate bound for his first full-time job as a newspaperman. I had a long way to grow, a long way to go, before I could, in my professor's words, "amount to something."

A Life Lesson Learned:

If I had to do it all over again, I would have majored in history. It would have been the most practical, useful, interesting pathway for my life and work. Even at a book or more a week of history and biography, I will never learn as much as I want. What once happened is so related to what can well happen again.

CHAPTER 5
THE EARLY NEWSPAPER YEARS

*"The two most important days in your life are the day you are born,
and the day you figure out why."*
–Author Mark Twain

B ack then you couldn't start at a better newspaper than
the *St. Petersburg Times*. It was legendary for giving young
journalists big responsibilities, big opportunities. I had
accepted the job at the *Times* early that year, but late that year
was wooed by the *Atlanta Journal-Constitution*—a bigger city
and ten bucks more a week. I was tempted. But my father said,
"You gave your word. You need to keep it." So I did. Bobbie and
I started married life in St. Petersburg at ninety-five dollars a
week; minus taxes and Social Security, my take-home pay was
seventy-nine dollars.

If we could make ten thousand dollars a year by the time we
were thirty, we reasoned, we should be just fine.

Our rent, on the second floor of an apartment ten blocks south
of the paper, was sixty-five dollars a month. We had a new
car—a dark blue Volkswagen Beetle, sticker price $1,595—
because Bobbie had received two thousand dollars in the past
few months, the legacy of her late father who died when she
was six.

Roberta and I were "kids" at age twenty-one when we were
married in 1963. Almost immediately, we were expecting a
baby. Between the second and third months of pregnancy she
had a terrible case of German measles; we were told there
could be significant, even staggering, consequences for our
child, and for us. We heard all sorts of advice about what to do.

But we never considered anything except hoping for the best. We were optimistic people at the dawn of our lives together. Faith, of course, had much to do with this.

David III was born the next October.

By then, I was off to a strong start at work, having already received a raise from $95 to $105 a week. It was the only money coming into our home. Roberta didn't have a paying job. We had enough money. Just enough, if we watched every nickel. After baby David arrived, the landlady of our second-floor apartment, compassionately and without our asking, lowered the monthly rent from $65 to $55. It helped.

Young David walked late and talked late. His speech was mostly incomprehensible to all but his parents for the first few years. We were worried, but retained our own hoping-for-the-best innocence. David would outgrow any problems, we reasoned.

Meanwhile, I had a job to worry about.

At the *Times*, I was given a mixture of editing and reporting assignments.

By the time I was twenty-five, I was telegraph editor, a title that now sounds antiquated, but meant that I was in charge of the first section of the paper, the one devoted to national and international news.

The top person at the paper was Nelson Poynter. In my job, I had almost nightly access to Mr. Poynter. He was a bow-tied little man—gentle and thoughtful—but nonetheless intimidating to someone four decades younger and someone who had achieved nothing yet. (Even almost four decades after his death, I cannot imagine calling him "Nelson.")

Mr. Poynter was devoted to quality and passionate about informing readers, and the paper had access to an abundance of news services—*The New York Times*, the *New York Herald Tribune*, *The Washington Post–Los Angeles Times* wire, the Associated Press, United Press International—plus bureaus in Washington, DC, and the state capital of Tallahassee.

The words "Florida's Best Newspaper" appeared just below the Page One masthead. The paper won its first Pulitzer in 1964 for uncovering the financial shenanigans in building the Florida Turnpike.

As editor of the A section, I came into nearly nightly contact with Mr. Poynter, who had strong feelings about what was news and what was not, and what was truly important and what was not. In mid-evening, just about 8:30, he would call in. "What's going on?" he would ask me. "Nothing much, Mr. Poynter" would have been unacceptably inane. The man wanted *the news.* That's why he owned the paper. He cared about the world we lived in.

Some people in conservative St. Petersburg referred to him as "a communist," which he was not. Nor was he a socialist. Rather he was a man of the world with great human and journalism values. Never provincial, he understood the importance of local news, but he also saw the whole world as "local," too. There was nothing "small-town" about Nelson Poynter.

He knew enough about business to hire the best people in those departments of the paper, too. Mr. Poynter knew he could afford the very best journalism if the *Times* were successful in advertising and circulation. It was. He was the farsighted executive who set up the process that keeps the paper, now called the *Tampa Bay Times*, in its rare and independent status. He was the man who established profit-sharing before most anyone else in newspapers or anyplace else.

The *Times* was progressive for those times, but by today's standards not what would be regarded as "enlightened." We did have coverage by two black reporters, but most of their work appeared in a special "Negro news page" that only went to the black community. (One of those two reporters, Sam Adams, went on to cover the Civil Rights Movement and later became a highly regarded journalism professor.) Women were mostly second-class citizens at the *Times.* They made less, had lesser jobs, and precious little path to greater responsibility and money. Anne Rowe Goldman quickly comes to mind. Hugely talented, she was in charge of the women's and feature sections with a staff of both women and men. A person this talented could have been the editor of the whole paper, but not back then.

In those days, the *Times* was ahead of "the pack" in professionalism, but—like all of us—needed to evolve. Though the *Times*, like all newspapers, struggles as a business now, it did remarkably well for decades. Some of that was due to its growing market on Florida's Suncoast, meaning that the best journalism could be afforded, and the best young journalists attracted. Some of its success can be traced to Mr. Poynter's larger view of the paper's mission as vital in the building of community and country—and a better world.

The newspaper business, if you wanted to "get ahead" in those times, had some of the characteristics of the parish priesthood. If you want to become a bishop, you had better be prepared to move around a good bit. (Until I went to Detroit in 1978, when I was thirty-six, my longest stint at any newspaper was four years.) I had a full appetite for more responsibility, and my father had always told me, "Be in charge if you can. It's more fun." (Not always true, I came to discover.) After three years at the *Times*, I began to be recruited by other newspapers—twice by *The Washington Post*, one of the perceived "holy grails" of American newspapering. I turned *The Post* down both times.

Aware of this, Bob Haiman, the managing editor, only five years older than I, called me into his office for a chat. "Why would you want to leave us?" he asked. "We are giving you more responsibility, and more pay."

Pay, I told him, was important, but people need more than that. A word of praise from time to time about my work would do wonders, I told him. From that day forward, he told me how well I was doing, how much I was valued. It occurred more frequently than seemed justified to me, and I left for *The Washington Post* the next time they asked me.

I like and admire Bob Haiman, who had a distinguished newspaper career at the *St. Pete Times* and its companion Poynter Institute for training journalists all over the country.

Maybe it was just me; I did want to be tested at a bigger, even more prominent newspaper. Nonetheless, those moments stayed with me as a great reminder about "appreciating" people. For the best part of my life and work, I have tried to apply that lesson, personally and professionally. Honest praise is a powerful incentive to do even better work.

It was mid-1967 when I took that job at *The Post*.

Not long after arriving in D.C., Bobbie and I saw a small story in a weekly newspaper in suburban Maryland. The National Institutes of Health was looking for mothers and offspring of the last great German measles epidemic—that is, the one we had gone through. Ultimately, NIH tested 125 mothers and 125 offspring (one of those being David III). He turned out to be just one of only two children with no profound deficits. They did find scar tissue behind his eyes and a problem hearing some sounds. They told us where help for David would be available. For the next several years, he had speech therapy at an Easter Seal clinic. Later he was graduated with high honors from the University of Michigan, went on to law school at Notre Dame, and today is an appellate lawyer in New York.

That we were able to access help and take advantage of "the system" made a great difference in David's future. Every parent deserves that chance. Every child deserves the real chance to fulfill his or her potential. My passion for what years later became my full-time work for children started here, I can see now. Without realizing it, I was already on the path toward the most meaningful chapter of my life.

Our second child, daughter Jennifer, also born in St. Petersburg, faced her own great challenge in adulthood. In her thirties, a social worker in Tallahassee, Florida, she was married to Jesse for nine years; then he died suddenly and accidentally. Two years after that great family tragedy, she fell in love with Walter Prather, a psychologist. Now they have two beautiful children, Mary and David. Mary was born in July 2003, and we had long planned to take all our children to Italy that Christmas. Might baptism at the Vatican be possible for Mary? (I have lived my life thinking just almost anything is possible.) I had been to St. Peter's before, had never seen a baptismal font there, but surely there must be at least one in a church that seats more than eighty-five hundred. There was. It took me almost five months to arrange, but the baptism came to pass in St. Peter's three days after Christmas in 2003. As for Christmas Eve, all in our family were there for the Mass broadcast around the world. Our pew was just three rows from the famous Bernini altar. The Vatican videographers, broadcasting the two-hour Mass around the world, could capture only so many moments of Pope John Paul II, the procession of Cardinals, the choir. Mary Katharine Prather—like all babies, cuter at five months old than at birth—is on that video three times. Decades from now, she will be able to see herself there. Her equally special brother David's beautiful baptism was in Tallahassee, Florida.

I was just twenty-five when I went to *The Washington Post*—on the news desk to which stories and pictures flowed, where pages were designed and headlines written. My boss was Dave Laventhol, later the publisher of *Newsday* and the *Los Angeles Times* and as creative an editor as I ever knew.

Ben Bradlee—the best-known newspaper editor of his time, who came to be a legend for his newsroom leadership in uncovering the scandal of Watergate that led to President Nixon's resignation—was executive editor of the paper. The also legendary Gene Patterson, toughened up in General George Patton's tank corps in World War II, was the managing editor. The biggest stories in my years at *The Post*—1967–69—were the Vietnam War and the 1968 assassinations of Dr. Martin Luther King Jr. and Robert F. Kennedy. Dr. King's death brought massive civil disturbances in Washington, and I went home after 1 a.m. many nights passing rifle-bearing soldiers stationed corner after corner. Ten days after the riots, a Sunday, it was safe enough to take Bobbie and our two children, ages two and four, to the heart of the worst disturbances. We could still smell tear gas.

These were years of disillusion and dissent, riot and rebellion in these United States. The antiwar movement was growing. The country was divided. Big cities were in flames. Troops had to be called out to keep order. President Johnson, then Nixon came under siege. Gov. George Wallace of Alabama, a serious presidential contender, was shot and paralyzed. Symbols of hope—MLK and RFK—were assassinated. The whole country seemed to be coming apart. It is difficult to know where you are in history when you are living it.

On October 21, 1967, on my day off, Bobbie and I—and one hundred thousand others—witnessed firsthand the March on the Pentagon. As a newspaperman, seeking to be "objective," I would not have participated in this anti-Vietnam War protest, or any demonstration—and never did. "Objectivity" in the newsroom took a hit five months later—March 31, 1968 to be exact—when Lyndon Johnson, under semi-siege for U.S. involvement in Vietnam, announced, "I shall not seek, and I will not accept" re-nomination as President of the United States. TV sets were on all over the newsroom. Paid-to-be-"objective" journalists were cheering. I knew how they felt, but was troubled by their reaction. A truly trying-to-be-objective journalist would never line up on anyone's "side."

Later in my *Post* tenure, Bradlee asked me to work as night editor of the "For and About Women" section of *The Post*. "Tell me what's going on there," he said, "and what you would recommend." What I recommended, in some part, led to the trailblazing "Style" section, launched on January 6, 1969. The modern feminist movement was catching hold, and newspaper editors were reconsidering their "women's pages."

"Style" was Bradlee's baby—and a defining moment in American journalism, followed in the next few years with similar approaches by most newspapers. Owner/publisher Katharine Graham was not in love with the early version. She was comfortable with what was already being done—the coverage of embassy parties, White House State Dinners, fashion. But Bradlee wanted, as he wrote in his memoir, a "section that would deal with how men and women lived—together and apart—what they liked and what they were like, what they did when they were not at the office.... We wanted to look at the culture of America as it was changing in front of our eyes. The Sexual Revolution, the drug culture, the Women's

Movement. And we wanted it to be interesting, exciting, different."

The longtime executive editor wrote that the skirmish over "Style" was the only major conflict he ever had with the *Post* publisher. " 'Damnit, Katharine,' " Bradlee said, "'Get your finger out of my eye. Give us six weeks to get it right, and then if you don't like it, we'll talk.'"

I remember vividly my own decision, as news editor of the just-launched "Style," to run a photograph of Bunny Mellon, played big on the front of that section, accompanied by a word portrait of the heiress and close friend of Kay Graham. That picture seemingly showed every line in her face. It was *the* Bunny Mellon—but certainly not the picture Mrs. Mellon would have liked us to run. Nor would have her good friend Mrs. Graham. The latter was really upset and could mostly only sputter that the picture wasn't "good journalism." I say that with great respect for Mrs. Graham. She was a terrific newspaper leader in the same pantheon as Nelson Poynter, Dave Laventhol, Ben Bradlee, Gene Patterson, and Knight Ridder's Jim Batten, Alvah Chapman, and Lee Hills.

As news editor of "Style," I saw every story before it ran. I edited some of the best people in the business, among them:

- Paul Hume, the classical music reviewer who in the decade before I arrived disparaged the singing of Harry Truman's pianist daughter and received the President's celebrated response: "Someday I hope to meet you. When that happens you'll need a new nose, a lot of beefsteak for black eyes, and perhaps a supporter below!"

- Sally Quinn, who came to "Style" with no background in journalism but brought with her the eyes, ears, and writing flair of the very best newsroom people. She wrote profiles of Washington's most fascinating people. She and Ben Bradlee were married in 1978 and remained so until his death in 2014.

- Nicholas von Hoffman, a star feature writer and columnist who wrote a major series on the hippie movement and the Haight-Ashbury scene. What he sent me contained far more opinion and personal judgment than I thought journalistic convention allowed. My editing made him angry enough to quit long-distance from San Francisco. At age twenty-seven, I was scared; on my watch I had caused a "star" to depart. Bradlee told me not to worry. "That's Nick. He'll be back." He was.

At *The Post*, I learned from the best, and learned that I could keep up with the best. The days were long, especially as we launched that pioneering "Style" section; not a few nights I would be put up at a nearby hotel, so as to be ready for the next more-than-full day. Most nights I was able to come home. We didn't have a lot of money, but we had enough to raise David III and Jennifer, pay rent that was four times what we had paid in St. Petersburg and, eventually, buy our first home for twenty thousand dollars. No mansion, it was nonetheless ours.

Our semblance of stability was threatened when *The Post*—beset by years of lousy labor relations—was struck by the unions. I was left without choices: I *had* to have a job, *and* I *had* to go on strike because Newspaper Guild union membership was required. That would mean no pay, only union benefits of thirty dollars a week, and we already had used up most every dollar we had saved from St. Petersburg. The strike turned out to last just days, but we couldn't know that when it started. I went to see Nelson Poynter in his nearby office at *Congressional Quarterly*, which he also owned. "You can work here for however long the strike lasts" he said, "and we will pay you whatever you are making at *The Post*." What a relief. What a lesson in how to treat people.

It was 1967, and I was moving along nicely at one of America's premier newspapers. But someone else came calling: Gregory Favre, the high-quality managing editor of the *Dayton Daily News* and about to become the editor of *The Palm Beach Post*. A half-dozen years older than I, he was—like me—a driven newsman. He needed a managing editor to run the day-to-day newsroom, and I wanted more responsibility.

The South Florida paper had been sold to Cox Enterprises by Perry Publications, John Perry's collection of mediocre mid-size Florida newspapers. (Mr. Perry had far more passion for building miniature submarines than he did for good journalism.) The West Palm Beach–Palm Beach area was growing quickly and becoming more diverse. A county then of more than three hundred thousand people, today it is five times larger.

In 1969, Bobbie and I started all over again, absorbing a pay cut from Washington so I could run a whole newsroom. We had enough money to buy a home with a thirty-year mortgage, and took with us a wooden jungle gym that I had won, in lieu of money, at a late-night poker game in Washington. In West Palm, we hired an almost entirely new staff. Most all of us were young and blissfully unaware of what we couldn't do. The paper was aggressive in a town unused to assertive journalism. Off work, we liked being with each other, too. Poker games were year-round; so, too, was softball. I kept my black Rocky Colavito glove for decades.

In my two years there, the paper won a number of national awards, including an Ernie Pyle and a Pulitzer and the first ever Robert F. Kennedy Award, much of it for coverage of migrant labor exploitation—a modern version of semi-slavery—in the rich black soil of western Palm Beach County. We also published a massive project on the scourge of drug addiction. Not a metropolitan daily by any measure, we acted like one, even sending our own reporter, Kent Pollock, to cover the war in Vietnam.

I never had run a newsroom before, and I was learning how to do it. We had plenty of money to spend, a good market in which to do it, and good stories to chase.

My management style was nothing I would brag about today. I didn't know any better. I was young, and it was mostly "my way or the highway," meaning I am sure that some people were told to leave who should have had more of a chance to understand and fix what they could have done better. "My way" was a lousy motivator of people, but it would take me a few more years—until Charlotte in the middle Seventies—before that lesson took. More on that later....

In November 1970, Bobbie and I went to the Associated Press Managing Editors convention. For that week in Honolulu, on the Hawaiian island of Oahu, we left at home young David and Jennifer, ages six and four. We missed them terribly. Within four days, we were trying to figure out how to get back home early. But we couldn't afford to change our plane schedule. When we came home, it was clear they both felt somewhat abandoned. In the years to come, as soon as we could afford the whole family traveling together, we took them with us, and they met people and had experiences they wouldn't have otherwise. I was coming to realize, first with my own children, what all children need.

In Honolulu, Larry Jinks, the well-known news executive of the *Miami Herald* and what was then called Knight Newspapers, asked to meet with me. He was clearly on the lookout for talent. We spent a couple of hours on a park bench talking about newspapers and our families, and he followed up after both of us returned home.

The other memory from that park bench is strolling servicemen, holding hands with wives and sweethearts, on leave from war-torn Vietnam. When Bobbie and I were married at the end of 1963, married men received a draft deferment. As the war went on, and more troops were called up, that marriage deferment was eliminated, but deferments still went to those with children. We had children. (In those years, I believed in the war, and wrote a letter to the besieged President Johnson supporting his leadership. He turned out to be wrong; I was, too. Vietnam was a national tragedy for the more than fifty-eight thousand Americans killed and three hundred thousand wounded, and their families, and for all of us.)

A month later, December 1970, deeply aware of the now-competitive *Palm Beach Post* just sixty-five miles up the road from Miami, Larry Jinks asked me to come to Miami to discuss Knight Newspaper opportunities. I met the brass in Miami, then was dispatched to Detroit to talk with Lee Hills, one of the best newspaper leaders in the country—someone who had learned shorthand to be a better, more accurate reporter— and someone who served for decades as the right hand of John S. Knight, at the pinnacle of a great newspapering enterprise. A serious, shy, and precise man, and an innovative and honorable leader, Lee Hills had one of America's most distinguished journalism careers, highlighted by a Pulitzer and other honors. Just to talk with him was, for me an honor.

That evening, I went out to the Detroit Press Club bar with the *Detroit Free Press*'s executive editor, Kurt Luedtke, one of Knight Newspaper's most brilliant journalism executives. (After departing newspapers, he wrote the screenplays for *Absence of Malice* and *Out of Africa*, the latter for which he received an Oscar.)

Larry Jinks had told me that the initial Knight opportunity would be in Philadelphia at the mostly street-sold tabloid *Philadelphia Daily News*. Kurt's counsel was this: "Turn that down.... Wait a few months, and you can do great things with me at the *Free Press*."

So much for good advice. The next day I was in Philadelphia to meet with Editor Rolfe Neill.

A Life Lesson Learned:

Some people know how to "work the system." Many do not—sometimes because of barriers of culture or language or socioeconomic status, or simply being intimidated by bureaucratic telephone voices sending people "somewhere else" to get help. I always thought I was "entitled" to reach anyone and get help. It made an enormous difference in getting help for our own family, beginning with David III's German measles challenge. Everyone is "entitled" to the basics of decency and service. Everyone. Insist on such.

CHAPTER 6
THE PHILADELPHIA STORY

*"The more that you read, the more things you will know.
The more that you learn, the more places you will go."*
–Dr. Seuss

In 1971, age twenty-nine, I joined Knight Newspapers as assistant to the editor (becoming, a few months later, managing editor) of the *Philadelphia Daily News*. The editor was Rolfe Neill, who had as quick a mind as anyone I have known in journalism. He was a bear on the "little things"—many of them actually not so little—that give a newspaper a better chance to connect with readers. It was here, for instance, that I learned the power of "localness." To the reader in Philadelphia an earth tremor in Pennsylvania can be bigger news than a death-and-destruction earthquake overseas. It was here that we—the first to do so in the country—not only reviewed the movies but told the reader how much sex and violence there was in that film (something I wanted to know on behalf of my own children). We needed every edge we could get at the *Daily News*, where we were a distant third place in circulation and had no Sunday paper. By the end of my tenure there—1971–75—we had gained circulation while both the *Bulletin* and *Inquirer* had lost readers.

Philadelphia is where I learned to compete—really compete. Anyone growing up with eight brothers and sisters will either compete or wilt. No one in our family ever wilted.

Even in those days, in the early Seventies, the newspaper business was in significant evolution, even if we couldn't see that then. Evening newspapers had been dominant for decades, especially in big northern factory towns like

Philadelphia and Detroit. By late afternoon, the "man of the house" was home from his factory job and, stereotypically, ready to sit in his easy chair, maybe smoking a pipe, and reading a newspaper while "Mom" made supper. Most cities of size still had two newspapers, but by now frequently with the same owner. Philadelphia, in contrast, still had three newspapers—the morning *Inquirer* and the afternoon *Daily News*, both owned by Knight Newspapers, and the locally owned evening *Bulletin* known for its long-running advertising campaign, "In Philadelphia, nearly everybody reads the *Bulletin*." (Ultimately, no one read the *Bulletin*. It died in 1982.)

Big cities with significant mass transit—Philadelphia and New York being examples—could support smaller-size newspapers called "tabloids" such as the *Daily News*. A tabloid was much easier to hold for someone squished between two other potential readers on a train or a trolley or subway. Unlike most newspapers, such as the *Inquirer* and the *Bulletin*, the *Daily News* had no home delivery; instead it was sold by hawkers or in vending machines.

The *Daily News*, billed then by the brilliance of Rolfe Neill as the "People Paper," was aimed at blue-collar workers and others who could be attracted by a headline in big type on the front page and content within that included a great sports section, a stable of provocative columnists, fine writing, editorials that didn't pussyfoot around, and coverage that ranged from the serious to scandals. We had only a fraction of the reporters and editors and photographers that the *Inquirer* and *Bulletin* could bring to bear. But if you don't need to be *them*—that is, your competitors—you could do things the others didn't do, or wouldn't do. One example: a front-page *Daily News* photograph of legendary tough guy and Police Commissioner Frank Rizzo, nightstick in his cummerbund, as he came from a black-tie dinner to the arrest, stripping and humiliation of lined-up members of the Black Panthers. Such a picture would never have run in either of our competitors.

The *Daily News* had to figure out how to do conventional journalism blended with the unconventional. On the one hand, we were clearly part of the Knight Newspapers group, known nationally for its quality journalism paid for by success in attracting readers and advertisers. (Though you had to live up to Knight Newspapers standards, decisions on content never were made in corporate headquarters, but always by local editors.) The *Daily News* wasn't trying to be—and wouldn't try to be—the sensationalized *National Enquirer*. On the other hand, with a staff less than a third of our competitors', we had to do things *they* weren't or wouldn't.

Which brings me back to Frank Rizzo.

This larger-than-life figure—friend of the FBI's J. Edgar Hoover and lauded by President Richard Nixon—served as police commissioner during times of revolt and rebellion in American cities. People loved him, or despised him. "Hero to some, villain to others," as *The New York Times* said when he died in 1991. He twice was elected mayor in the Seventies—my time in Philadelphia. He had aspirations beyond being mayor of the "City of Brotherly Love." Governor of Pennsylvania was to be his next stop. But...

In 1973, Rizzo was enmeshed in an immense political feud with Pete Camiel, the Democratic Party boss in a machine-politics city. Camiel accused Rizzo of offering patronage to influence political candidates; Rizzo called him a liar. The *Daily News* asked both to take a lie detector test. Rizzo—perhaps thinking that as a longtime cop he was smarter than any machine— agreed. The *Daily News* hired a lie detector expert from Miami, and Rizzo failed the test. The two-line front-page headline—in the biggest type we had—said simply: *"Rizzo Lied, Test Shows."* Below was a picture of Rizzo strapped to the machine, with this quotation alongside: "If this machine says a man lied, he lied." Thus ended his chances of becoming governor.

The Lawrences loved this tempestuous town, which all too often did not live up to its long-lived label, "The City of Brotherly Love." Philadelphia was a great "news town," as newspaper people would say, meaning more than a fair share of misery and mayhem to cover. There was also much good for us to see and sample. Our family took full advantage of our years (1971–75) there. Bobbie returned to college, and finished her bachelor's in political science at Temple University. Our two children, David and Jennifer, were doing well in elementary school. We rented an apartment in suburban Lansdowne and later bought a home in Havertown. Travel to work was on the train—a great opportunity for reading on the way. Because the *Daily News* had no Sunday edition, the Lawrence family had a full weekend day to spend time in Philadelphia to visit Independence Hall, Betsy Ross's home, and other places that celebrated the beginning of our country. We took our children to the games of all four major sports teams. (Most of all, we loved the baseball Phillies. For years I kept a ball caught off the bat of future Hall of Famer Mike Schmidt.)

In Knight Newspapers, I was seen as somewhat of a "whiz kid," advancing far and fast in newspaper leadership, and no doubt a tad too full of myself at some moments. Like the time that John S. Knight—the great soul of Knight Newspapers, the "owner" before the company went public, and a Pulitzer recipient for his writings on Vietnam—wrote a column saying he couldn't vote for either Richard Nixon or George McGovern in 1972. I wrote him an impudent letter suggesting we all had to vote for someone. He responded, in writing, suggesting I should "grow up." I did. How foolish to act like a smarty-pants before a genuine giant of the business and a man forty-eight years my senior.

A good editor is a good "trainer" of talent, and I became one. In Philadelphia I was asked to take on John S. Knight III, only three years younger than I, as my assistant, and help him to "grow up," too. This brilliant young man was destined for a bright future, all the while burdened by having the name of one of the great figures of twentieth-century journalism. (Young Knight's father, Lt. John S. Knight Jr., was killed in France in the closing days of World War II.) A few months after I left Philadelphia, young John was stabbed to death in his Rittenhouse Square apartment. That tragedy stays with me.

We didn't go to Philadelphia thinking we'd be there a long time, and we weren't. But I cannot think of a place where I learned more about how to compete and how to grow up. But, now, said the bosses at Knight, it was time to go to Charlotte, North Carolina.

A Life Lesson Learned:

The first Henry Ford had a lot of junk in his soul—look it up if you don't know what I mean—but he had some wisdom, too, saying once: "Whether you think you can, or think you cannot—you're right." There is enormous power within each of us; it begins with believing in oneself. You'd be amazed at what you can do, but you have to try. Really try.

CHAPTER 7
TAKING IT PERSONALLY
IN CHARLOTTE

"I've learned that people will forget what you said, people will forget what you did, but people will never forget how you made them feel."

—Author Maya Angelou

It was not easy following god. Not the capital "G" God. James K. Batten was not an actual deity. But he was a deeply loved leader in journalism, rising to be the chief executive officer and chairman of Knight Ridder, the country's second-largest newspaper group (behind only Gannett) and widely regarded as the company that most emphasized high-quality journalism.

Jim Batten began his newspaper career in 1957 at *The Charlotte Observer* as a cub reporter (who wrote in longhand because he couldn't yet type). He returned in 1972 as the *Observer*'s executive editor, the top post in the newsroom. After just three years, he was asked to join Knight Ridder's corporate staff in Miami. Loving what he was doing, and having strengthened the newsroom staff, he was reluctant to depart Charlotte. But the leadership in Miami convinced him that his new responsibilities could protect and enhance the ability to do good journalism in not just one newspaper, but many.

That meant a successor would be needed in Charlotte, and I was recruited from Philadelphia.

I knew and respected Jim Batten (and came, in fact, to love him.). But I had no idea how tough it would be to follow in his footsteps.

The Observer newsroom staff worshipped Jim. They were convinced, however naively, that he would be their inspirational leader for many years to come. He had thought the same. Now, seemingly all of a sudden, he was gone. I arrived in August 1975 at age thirty-three to a staff quite certain I was no Jim Batten. They were right.

Earning the staff's trust would be a struggle. While I was committed to aggressive, high-quality journalism, I had to do much more than saying such to convince a staff that was paid for asking good questions and being healthily skeptical. Jim came from southern Virginia and the Carolinas, had begun his reporting career at *The Observer*, and had a convincingly mellow southern tongue that blended gentleness and toughness. I spoke in a way that didn't feel "Charlotte." I had much to learn about the people of the newsroom and the people of the communities we served, but those in the newsroom had much to learn, too.

In my earliest days, I met with every reporter, editor, and photographer. I wanted to know them, and I wanted them to know me. A newspaper is part of the community—and should be—and I had to learn the communities we covered. I insisted that the staff learn with me. I dragged all sorts of newsroom people out of the office on the premise that there is precious little to learn at your desk. Together, we visited textile mills (a principal industry in the Piedmont area of the Carolinas), religious leaders (we were in the Bible Belt), political and civic leaders, and bankers (Charlotte was a New South banking capital). Some of the staff didn't like these "tours"—thinking it all too boosterish—but they (and I) needed to learn, and we did. Our coverage of the communities we served became deeper and more connected.

I shared Jim Batten's journalistic values, and I had his toughness, but was less of a gentleman about it. (Some level of toughness goes with any real leader's responsibilities.) Early on, I had to fire a popular *Observer* book editor and restaurant reviewer who turned out to be a little too popular. It was discovered that he was privately advising restaurant owners; on at least one occasion, he gave a very positive review to one of those restaurants he had advised. My style is to be open, to be straightforward, to tell you what I am doing. That wasn't the way most newspapers handled things; dirty laundry wasn't washed in public. But I thought readers deserved to know what preceded and justified the decisions we made. I wrote a column explaining the dismissal: "We live in a time when many institutions (including newspapers) are being reassessed and individuals' integrity is being questioned.... We must make sure that we at *The Observer* avoid any conflicts and even the appearance of potential conflict."

At times, looking back now, I could be too tough. However sure I was that I cared about the people who worked with and for me, it didn't mean *they* knew it. Many, it turned out, did not know. Eventually it got back to me that reporters and editors—quietly, covertly—had begun gathering signatures to form a union.

Alarmed, I delivered that news to my boss, Publisher Rolfe Neill, who had come to *The Observer* a few months after me. I wanted empathy. I wanted comfort. I wanted him to say, "I know how hard you work; you don't deserve this." I got none of that. "You need to take this 'personally,' " he told me. He said it was about *me* and my leadership. I took it that way, and I have been forever since well served by that. I had to change how I dealt with people. If I truly cared about people, people had to know that and *know* it as real.

I learned. Learned the value of genuine praise. Learned that I needed to listen more. Learned that I needed to order less, and trust more. None of this happened overnight; it couldn't have. But, eventually, I had learned more about the people who worked with and for me, and they had learned more about me. The respect was mutual. Trust had been established.

That union movement never came to a vote.

~~~

It was a good time to be in journalism. We were profitable, with the financial underpinnings to afford increasing excellence. The better the journalism, the more readers and, consequently, more advertising dollars.

There were no "sacred cows." There wasn't a subject we couldn't take on. That included word portraits of the most powerful people in town, and we did such stories regularly. But what about profiling Publisher Neill? That would be a no-win proposition for the top newsroom editor—me. Rolfe didn't want to be written about; who could blame him? I wouldn't have liked it myself. But how could I tell the city desk that our own top boss was the exception on the list of those we could cover? So when the city desk came up with the idea that we ought to profile Rolfe Neill, I didn't say, "No." But I surely knew that this story spelled trouble.

Whatever great positives Rolfe had—and there were many— there was no way to write an honest profile of anyone (with the potential exception of Mother Teresa) without turning up some things that the subject wouldn't like. In this instance, one of those was church attendance in a city where I can remember being asked repeatedly, "Where do you go to church?" Presbyterian, Baptist, and Methodist churches were the most acceptable answers. Rolfe Neill had Presbyterian origins but little detectable devotion. "I don't think there is a God, but I really don't know," he was quoted as saying in the piece. He didn't much like the story—too long, too much detail, some negatives (and mostly positives)—but he put up with it. Jack Knight, at the summit of what had become Knight Ridder, made it clear that pursuing this story was "a damned fool idea." And in some ways it was. But it is a tribute to Mr. Knight and to the journalism ethos he fostered and to Rolfe Neill's (he was my boss, remember) that the story could be reported, written, and run. There was nothing "sensational" in that piece. It profiled a powerful man—smart as a whip and distrusted by some for his smoothness—who wasn't perfect, but better, no doubt, than most of us.

Meanwhile, we were in the same metropolitan area as Jim and Tammy Faye Bakker, the televangelists with a theme park. Their ministry ran under the banner of The PTL Club, standing for "Praise The Lord." I took reporters and editors to meet them, and subsequently we came to cover them closely. Some years later, the *Observer* won a Pulitzer for its coverage of PTL and its conduct that came more closely to be defined as "Pass The Loot." The Bakker business ended up in a scandal involving adultery and paid sex, and tax fraud, for which he served five years in prison.

Billy Graham, native of Charlotte, was a quite different sort of Christian. America's best known preacher—a spiritual adviser to Presidents—and widely admired. He "saved" millions of souls in "crusades" on six continents. (My wife Bobbie and I went to hear him when he came to the University of Florida in the early Sixties. We declined stepping down the stadium steps to be saved because both of us were comfortable with the beliefs we had.)

Reverend Graham was a prodigious fund-raiser. But exactly how many millions did he raise? How were those dollars spent? For months *Observer* reporters pursued answers. Our major investigative series showed that the Billy Graham Evangelistic Association had an awful lot of money, and wasn't keen on telling the public how much because that wouldn't help to raise even more. There was nothing illegal here, but nor was it a shining example of Christian transparency. That series, in the summer of 1977, caused a firestorm in the *Observer*'s circulation territory. Angry readers cancelled subscriptions and dominated talk radio.

With reader heat at a fever pitch, I went literally to the mountaintop to see Billy Graham in his compound at Montreat in Western North Carolina. I asked a lot of questions, took copious notes, and wrote about it all. Readers turned out to be most interested in the answer to one question in particular, and it had to do with Elvis Presley. That great entertainer, his later years no soft ballad of life, had just died, at age forty-two, probably from an overdose of prescription medicine. Like tens of millions of Americans, I loved his music and, in fact, had seen every one of his thirty-one movies. "Where do you suppose Elvis Presley is now, Dr. Graham?" I asked. The Reverend, acknowledging Elvis's sometimes dissolute later years, believed in a forgiving God and thought Elvis must be in Heaven. That comment turned out to be "news" picked up by the Associated Press and headlined around the world.

That fall, I invited Ruth and Billy Graham to sit in on a news meeting at the *Observer* where top editors discussed what stories were "working" that day and what "Page One" might look like. He enjoyed it immensely, coming away with a deeper appreciation for the role of good journalism. While our stories clearly had stung him, he didn't take it personally; instead, he made sure that the finances of the Billy Graham Evangelistic Association became far more transparent. (A turning-the-other-cheek postscript: A dozen years later, about to leave Detroit for Miami, I was honored at a community dinner attended by more than eight hundred people; Billy Graham agreed to be the featured speaker. I kept in touch with Reverend Graham all the years since, receiving a Christmas message every year.)

In those same years, we wrote countless stories as Charlotte and Mecklenburg County wrestled with desegregation and the Supreme Court's *Swann* decision on busing schoolchildren. (Once again, the constant theme of what is best for children touched my life and work.) We moved from a "For and About Women" section to one that was more embracing of everyone and called "Carolina Living." We took on the police chief by publishing an investigative series revealing the destruction of evidence related to allegations of an illegal program of police wiretapping. That series triggered a thirteen million dollar libel suit filed by the chief, but our reporting eventually was confirmed, and the suit dropped.

There were many good days in Charlotte, but not all. By way of example, there was the *Observer* reader in neighboring Shelby (a conservative town known for running union organizers out of the textile mills) who wrote to Jim Knight. James L. Knight was deeply conservative and the businessman of the Knight brothers (Jack being the journalist). The reader was concerned, he told Mr. Knight, as to whether the new editor—that being I—might be a "Communist." Jim Knight wrote back saying he sort of wondered the same thing, with an indicated carbon copy to me. I was enraged. How could I do my job with this sort of "support"? Jim Batten, then the vice president of news for Knight Ridder, calmed me down, making it clear I had his and the company's full support. "That's just Jim Knight," I remember Batten saying.

Overall, we loved our three years in Charlotte, where our third child, Amanda Katherine, was born. Today Amanda is married to Bailey. They live outside Washington, DC, where she lobbies for local governments in multiple states, and he leads the communications office for a major trade association. Everything went fine with their firstborn, Julia. Their second, Katherine, spent her early days in intensive care. Today both are growing up beautifully, but it was another reminder of life's challenges for every family, another example that would serve me in my later mission.

In Charlotte, I turned thirty-five and quit smoking—three packs of Larks a day—to give me a better chance of seeing our children, David and Jennifer, and then Amanda (and two more later) into adulthood. (I was intense enough without cigarettes.) Bobbie was in the final stages of a graduate program in urban administration.

Much would be interrupted if I departed, but I was being told it was time to leave after only three years—the same tenure given to Jim Batten, my predecessor in Charlotte. (In newspaper management of that time—in companies that owned many newspapers—change was the only constant.) I was told I was needed in Detroit where the challenges were immense, and that was that. Move we would. Knight Ridder's *Detroit Free Press* was engaged in an old-fashioned newspaper war with the larger *Detroit News*, and something—soon—had to give.

Leaving Charlotte was tough for everyone, though least of all for me. We would all be starting over—in a bigger city, at a bigger newspaper with bigger challenges. I would be anchored by a loving family.

Charlotte was where we had our first real sense of community. "Neighbors" meant something extra in Charlotte. Better be fully dressed at home—a neighbor might bring over a chocolate cake in any hour of daylight. We paid $72,000 for our home, worried it was probably too much, and sold it for

$102,000 three years later. Look on the internet today, and the market estimate for that home is $2.2 million. (We never should have sold!) The living room was eighteen by thirty-four feet, and a beautiful park was on the other side of the road. I remember the bars on the windows of baby Amanda's room, installed by a previous owner in response to the Lindbergh infant kidnapping in 1932.

As I departed for my next stop, the *Detroit Free Press*, *The Observer*'s beloved Kays Gary wrote a column in which there were these words:

> We had heard that he was a giant killer, a tough young man of thirty-three. Yes, in came David, a roly-poly dynamo with a puckish smile. This was a giant killer? He was tough, yes, with principles of truth and fairness: inexhaustible in his efforts to know and understand every member of the staff, every facet of this city and region. His office door remained open. He searched out critics of *The Observer*. He welcomed staffers' complaints, even from people long ago tagged as "nuts." Compassion? In no individual have I encountered more of it.
>
> Lawrence responded with respect to all segments of interest, public and private, with staggering energy, will, and optimism, and not a trace of deviousness. Surely, no one would ever say, after a session with Lawrence, "What did he mean by that?" He brought to *The Observer* a liveliness and response to the interests of young readers. He sought to make it serve people and their interests wherever they lived, despite the differences in metropolitan and rural areas. He is a fearless commander in baggy pants, a scholar of unquenchable thirst in seeking reasons, answers and understanding of individuals and movements. As you may have gathered, in three too-short years, we came to love and respect the guy in a way that finds words weak. He gave us more than pride. He enlarged our self-esteem and at the same time allowed us to discover the strength of humility.

Saturday he told us. Grown people cried. Thank God
I wasn't alone. Some of us are angry; not at Knight
Ridder, for he wasn't moved. He made the choice. Not
at him because, well, there is no way to be angry with
Dave. But we are losing more than an editor and friend.
We are losing a Catholic father and Jewish mother,
Bobbie, and their three adored children (David, age
fourteen, Jennifer, age twelve, and Amanda, age two) who
represent a triumph of love and family that all humanity
struggles to attain, although sometimes too weakly. We
wish him well.

Have you no soul, Detroit? Isn't it enough we're buying
your cussed cars. If there was ever an imbalance of trade,
this is it. In your favor.

That piece meant a lot to me (though I could have done without
"roly-poly!").

In a farewell column, I wrote, "It's hard to say 'goodbye.' ...
Charlotte has been good to us."

My life for decades meant I would need to invest myself deeply
in every community in which I lived and worked—learning
everything I could, making as much difference as I could—and
then move on. It was the nature of the business then; I worked
for a big company and good people, people I trusted who had a
big say-so in deciding what was best for the business, and for
me. Bobbie and I and the children started over many times—
too many for the children and probably for Bobbie, too (though
I've always admired her adventurous spirit). It did give our
children extra resilience that would stand them in good stead
in adulthood. But I clearly remember our family's tougher
moments. When we left Charlotte, David III was fourteen and
settled into school and activities; Detroit would be his fifth
move. When I told him we would be moving once more, he
said, in pain, "It's not fair." It wasn't, I know.

Even if not the best time to go, I was going. In a November 21,
1978, note of commendation, Jim Batten had some nice things
to say about what had been accomplished in our relatively
brief stay in Charlotte.

"And now," he wrote, "Detroit."

A Life Lesson Learned:

If you really care about people, they need to know it. So often—
however good a person you might be—they really don't know
you really care about them. All people need to be needed,
wanted, fulfilled, and, yes, loved.

CHAPTER 8
DETROIT: WAR AND DIVERSITY

"I cannot believe that the purpose of life is to be 'happy.' I think the purpose of life is to be useful, to be responsible, to be compassionate. It is, above all, to matter; to count."
—Author Leo Rosten

Newspapering in Detroit would energize every gene of my competitive DNA. In the late Seventies, Knight Ridder's morning *Free Press* was locked in mortal combat with the afternoon and locally owned *Detroit News*. The *Free Press* and the *News*, two of the biggest newspapers in the country, each reached hundreds of thousands of readers every day of the week. When I look back to my eleven newspapering years there—1978–89—what comes to mind is a years-later front-page picture in the *Miami Herald* of a python and an alligator, embracing each other unto death in the Everglades.

By the time I arrived in 1978 as executive editor, the *Free Press* was barely making money, and the *News* doing little better. Keep this up, and one of those newspapers would be defunct; so, too, would be more than two thousand jobs. The competition was ultimately unsustainable, especially so for the shareholders of the public company that was Knight Ridder. Growth in earnings was the only acceptable corporate path forward. But how to make that happen? The field marshals at Knight Ridder in Miami for whom I worked weren't the surrendering sort. Nor was I, who became a general on the battlefield in Detroit. It was all-out war, an ever-escalating series of battles for readers and advertisers—and an increasing hit to the bottom-line. We had no obvious path forward, except to compete until we couldn't compete any more.

From that competition came superb journalism. The newsroom had to be on edge every day. Give "the enemy" no quarter. Encourage every news tip. Work your sources. Know your beat. Dig deeper. Ask every conceivable question. Then ask at least one more. Make one more phone call. Then another. Get the facts first, and get them right. Shoot the best pictures. (The *Free Press'* Taro Yamasaki won a Pulitzer in photography in those years.) Design a compelling front page every day. Write headlines that *insisted* the story would be read. Meet every deadline. A story that doesn't make it to the presses on time won't get to readers when they need the newspaper. That was especially true of sports. In a town obsessed with Tigers, Lions, Pistons, and Red Wings—and University of Michigan football—sports sold newspapers, especially when *your* team won. Indeed, the biggest sales bump the *Free Press* ever had—in more than a century and a half of service—was an extra eighty thousand papers the day after the baseball Tigers won the World Series in 1984.

It was intense. Exhilarating and exhausting.

No business can go on and on and on while losing money. But until we *had* to face that ultimate reality, readers would receive extraordinary, beat-your-pants-off journalism. I was a front-line, battle-hardened officer in the last great newspaper war in the country. Most days it was as much fun as you could have in the business—but accompanied by maybe mortal consequences.

Before the war was over, a lot of good journalism was done.

Years later, as I was about to leave the *Free Press* for Miami in 1989—with a going-away party in Tiger Stadium—a gifted *Free Press* writer named Patricia Edmonds wrote a profile of me that I didn't see until it appeared in the newspaper. It started this way:

> *Put David Lawrence Jr. in an after-work volleyball game and he'll dive for every shot, business suit be damned.*
>
> *Let another car try to cut ahead of his in traffic, and he'll see that car bashed before he'll let it in.*

Ask him to raise money for a cause and he'll roll up millions.

Or: Make him general in one of America's last great newspaper wars, and watch him fight as if for his own life.

Then tell him there's been a truce.

See if it's not like telling him to repeal his own heartbeat.

Your Honor, if it may please the Court, I stipulate to those facts and plead guilty. But there's more to the story—and more to me.

Those paragraphs serve as sort of summary of my eleven years at the *Free Press*. Arriving in 1978 as executive editor, I became publisher at the beginning of 1985 at the age of forty-two. That meant I was responsible not only for the news and editorial pages, but also for all the business operations, including advertising, marketing, circulation, production.

The newsroom would always be my first love, as it had been my father's. As I advanced in newspaper responsibilities, my proud father was eager to tell almost anyone about his son's success. His death in September 1983 meant that when I became publisher sixteen months later, my joy would be diminished by his earthly absence.

The month my father died, I left for a previously arranged thirteen-week Advanced Management program at the Harvard Business School. In preparation for that program, which Jim Batten thought I should attend, my summer mornings were spent with the *Free Press* comptroller teaching me to make sense of balance sheets and income statements.

I loved journalism, but all that business "stuff" scared me. My Harvard classmates—120 of them from thirty-three countries—gave me a deeper appreciation for the world and its cultures. But most of those classmates seemed to know far more than I about business. With a hunger to "catch up," at Harvard I studied after dinner until one every morning, and was up by five to dig into the "case studies" again. Six weeks into the program came my "Now I get it!" moment.

That Saturday morning I led a class discussion on something called the "internal rate of return"—that is, a way to calculate the attractiveness of a proposed investment. After the class, buoyantly proud of myself, I called Bobbie back home 725 miles away. "I can do this stuff!" I told her. Truth to tell— before then, and all the years after—I never cared that much about making money. I respected and honored the fact that the money made by the paper paid for the journalism. As publisher, I would have to care about revenues and profit margins, and I did. (A truer measure of my "appreciation" for money can be seen in the course of our marriage of more than a half-century. In any given year, I probably don't sign more than a half-dozen checks. Bobbie's capable handling of our own resources freed me for much else.)

In my early *Free Press* years, with Knight Ridder's full support, we opened several national bureaus, plus international bureaus in Eastern Europe and Africa (both places where many of our readers had interests and often family history). We strengthened business coverage, with a particular focus on cars in the "auto capital" of Detroit. Our features coverage became stronger; so did the depth and clout of our editorial pages. Sports, always vital, became stronger with the hiring of columnists Mike Downey and Mitch Albom, both big-league talents. Political coverage and columns were emphasized. At the core were elegant writing and hard-hitting local and state coverage.

The quality and composition of our newsroom staff became an emphasis for me. When I arrived in 1978, in a city more than two-thirds black, our newsroom staff of perhaps 225 journalists included a total of four minority staff members. (One of those four—an Asian American—insisted he was not a "minority.")

The newsroom, like every newsroom I've known, was peopled and led by mostly traditional "liberals"—good people, almost all non-Hispanic white, all quite sure they cared about everyone. But good intentions would never suffice to achieve a newspaper that genuinely covered the *whole* community. Even if I were the most thoughtful "white liberal" editor anywhere, if I told you that I knew what it was like to be "black" or a "woman" or much else, be very wary of me. Life has taught me that well-intentioned people frequently get in the way of real progress.

The best journalism requires coverage and commentary reflecting the full community. Really fine journalism is not only about problems and challenges, but also about people who inspire. That is both fair and journalistically honest.

With all that at the core of my optimist's soul, here are five things I insisted on for the *Free Press* newsroom:

- *No. 1: We would have a staff and management reflective of the community we served. We couldn't cover the whole community without people of many perspectives.*

- *No. 2: We would have no "quota" system; no one would be hired because she or he was of a certain color or gender.*

- *No. 3: We would hire only the highest-quality people, which would not necessarily mean the most experienced.*

- *No. 4: We would fill no vacancies unless and until we had diversity in our finalists—and we would need to think about promotions similarly.*

- *No. 5: Success would not be a "sink-or-swim" approach, but rather about extending a helping hand to a person who was not only new to us, but who might also be seen as somehow "different." Role models and mentors would be important.*

Lo and behold, we began to recruit and hire wonderful people whom we had not known of before. Those people, many of them minorities, began to tell other people that we could be a great place to do good journalism. That led us to more first-rate hires. By the time I departed the *Free Press*, we had the highest percentage of minorities as newsroom professionals of any urban newspaper in the country. One of those people was Robert G. McGruder, who came to the *Free Press* as deputy managing editor in 1986, seeing that we were serious about both people and journalism. Ultimately he became executive editor—the top newsroom position—and was among the first black people in that role in America.

Every difference I helped make happen goes back to my earliest years. Lawrences were taught to work hard, be fair, tell the truth, respect everyone, do no less than lead a life of meaning to yourself and others. Those lessons were underscored by growing-up memories—that aforementioned Klan march when I was a senior in high school, then as a student at the University of Florida riven by disagreements over desegregation.

Those lessons were complemented and undergirded by regularly reading history and biographies. History taught me that while people of goodwill are central to progress, real progress requires pushing and shoving, cajoling and coaxing—and then pushing some more, courteously if you can, not so courteously if the former doesn't lead to results. History reminded me that what seemed "radical" in one generation (suffrage, Social Security, Medicare) can become the accepted "American" foundation of a later generation.

Justice is the heritage of our family. In the late Thirties, my father was a member of the Interracial Relations Group at Manhattan College in New York City. Without being aware of that, in the Eighties I became a "life member" of the NAACP. In that decade I led a newspaper industry task force to increase minority representation, most especially in newsrooms. Subsequently I was honored for lifetime achievements with the Ida B. Wells Award and the National Association of Minority Media Executives Award. Today, I am on the board of trustees of Florida A&M University, one of this country's largest HBCUs ("historically black colleges and universities"). Because its mission is so vital, FAMU quickly became my favorite board work.

In the depths of my being, I have known some things for decades: Each of us remains, to some extent, a prisoner of our own prejudices (most often not realizing we have them). The faith or color or gender or nationality we know most about usually is our own. We build our biases based on what we have seen, what we have experienced, what we have been told, what we have read or learned. Too often, we have not dug deep enough to accumulate the wisdom to challenge our own prejudices. The best of us struggle all our lives with the human tendency to feel most comfortable with people like ourselves.

I came to know that my life did not provide an unabridged perspective on all that is important in this world. I came to believe in the essentiality of a pluralistic workplace and country—people of all colors, of all heritages and cultures, of all ages, men and women, able-bodied and not, of differing sexual orientation. Our souls need room for everyone—people with families and people without families, people who pray and people who do not, people with children in schools and those who do not have children in schools, people who fight for the environment and people who must fight for the essential basics of life, people who handle hammers, people who drive trucks, people who prepare food, people with power and people without power, people with means and people without means.

All of us.

As a student of history, I know that ours is a nation in which discrimination is not yet infrequent, where many people lack real opportunity for a fair share of reward and responsibility.

A real leader must ask himself or herself: How many good people might have stayed with us if we had worked harder to help them feel more welcome? How can we contribute to their personal and professional growth? Good people need to feel needed, wanted, fulfilled in their work, even loved. Money is important, but money is never what is most important to the best people.

In Detroit was born what came to be called "Dave Raves." These brief handwritten notes from me carried praise for perhaps a well-written story, tough investigative reporting, an "exclusive" or "scoop" that our competitor didn't have, a great headline, a "wow" of a picture, an artist's fine sketch, a masterful column. Or maybe securing a new advertiser, or working hard, and successfully, to retain an especially upset reader.

These notes came from my heart as well as my mind. I've always needed bosses to appreciate my work. When they did, I worked even harder. I wanted for others what I wanted for myself. *Real* praise needs to be *really* earned. Moreover, if I were going to criticize moments of failure—and I did—I also was obliged to compliment those who performed with special distinction. People need to know that they and their work are respected and appreciated, that they work at a place where they can grow and do their best work.

I still hear from people who have saved these notes for decades. By way of example, I quote from a letter I received from Ron Dzwonkowski, who worked for me at the *Free Press* in the Eighties, retiring in 2012 as the editorial page editor. It is shared with his permission:

> Sorting through and cleaning out stacks of old files, I came across a number of notes from you in that bold blue pen. Not all were what we used to call "Dave Raves." Some were critical and challenging.

> One was kind and understanding, sent while you were on a fellowship and had apparently learned of my hospitalization for alcoholism. I was expecting to be fired. (Just so you know, I remain a member in good standing of AA and devote time to helping others who are still sick and suffering.)

> But I write simply to say thank you—for hiring me, for not firing me, and for those handwritten notes that are so rare in this age of email and text messaging. I will keep several in my career scrapbook—and I will tell people that they came from a man who really cared.

That meant the world to me.

Not all moments were great. Couldn't be.

There were constant tangles with unions. None of our twelve unions were big believers in management's appraisal of financial realities. With the Republican National Convention coming to Detroit in 1980—a grand moment for hometown newspaper coverage of Ronald Reagan's nomination—the unions struck. They thought management would buckle. We didn't. That the *Free Press* couldn't publish for these key days was a crushing blow for everyone in the newsroom.

Another tough moment came two years later, in 1982. The DeVos family of Michigan—the Amway folks—was very upset about how we covered their schemes involving cross-border (Canada–U.S.) customs fraud. Here's how one *Free Press* story started: "Top officers of the Amway Corp. bilked Canada of tens of millions of dollars in customs duties since 1965 by concocting phony warehouse and sales receipts and by misrepresenting the nature of their U.S. operations." Amway went public with a threat to sue the *Free Press* for a half-billion dollars. That's an intimidating amount. Ultimately, the *Free Press* paid not a penny, and Amway paid twenty-eight million dollars to settle its criminal fraud problems.

Not only were there tough stories to write, but also tough decisions to be made. Gay couples were beginning to ask for the ability to run their couples announcements in the paper. The business-side leadership thought printing these would damage the newspaper. I decided to run them; that just seemed fair. Nothing erupted; life went on. Meanwhile, in the Auto Capital of the World, car dealers were upset about stories that gave readers advice as to how to get the best deals and how to play one dealer off another. Dealers, unsurprisingly, didn't want that sort of information shared and, thus, boycotted the paper for months. It cost us hundreds of thousands of dollars. Eventually they returned because a newspaper trusted by readers is a good place to sell cars.

And I faced a tough personal decision. Influential people in Michigan wanted me to run for the United States Senate. I took them seriously, and would have loved to have served. Bobbie thought I would be wounded deeply by the ugliness of a political campaign. She was convincing. Meanwhile, I was in demand elsewhere. Other newspapers were after me, most notably the Times Mirror chain to be both editor and publisher of the *Hartford Courant*. What attracted me was doing both jobs for a newspaper dominant in its home state of Connecticut. I was almost set to depart, but Jim Batten talked me out of it. If you have a boss as good as Jim Batten, it ought to be very hard to leave. It was too hard.

Becoming *Free Press* publisher at the beginning of 1985, I came into even greater daily contact with the area's financial, political, and cultural establishments. The newspaper was many things to many people, and the publisher was expected to be a community leader. I dove into those responsibilities—serving on some boards, deciding as a newspaper what we could support, opposing what we thought needed opposition, resisting pressure on our journalistic mission and values, raising money when asked to do so by worthy groups.

Not long after I became publisher, the director of the Detroit Zoo came to me. "I really need your help," Steve Graham said over breakfast at the Detroit Club. "You can say, 'No,' " he told me, "but you are going to have to say it twice." It wasn't a good time—once or twice—to ask me to do anything extra. I had more than enough to do. But at least I could give him a chance to explain. He said we need to think about animals differently, and chimps would be a good place to start. The Detroit Zoo hadn't unveiled a major new exhibit in at least two decades. Steve gave me a history lesson about the "old days" at the zoo with tutu-wearing chimpanzees performing on motorcycles and smoking cigars. Animals deserve to be treated with respect, he said, adding that what was really needed would be a natural-habitat exhibit where chimpanzees could be themselves.

I said, "No."

Two weeks later, we had breakfast again. I had done some reading, and was at least intrigued. (One of my strengths—it can be a weakness—is that I can get interested in almost anything.) "Is there any place where I can easily see what this might look like?" I asked. Well, Steve said, we could visit the natural-habitat zoo in Asheboro, North Carolina. We did that. By then I had learned enough to know this would be good for Detroit—and for chimpanzees. (If you respect animals, that tells me something good about you.) I was converted generally.

But how could I spend enough time to raise the necessary millions, and still fulfill my basic obligations to the *Free Press* and its people?

"You really ought to see the best in the world," Steve said. Where was that? Arnhem, in the Netherlands. If I went there, I also could do something I had long really wanted to do—see Anne Frank's hiding place in Amsterdam. How could I miss that? Before the trip, I read Jane Goodall's *The Chimpanzees of Gombe*. The acknowledged world expert on the topic, she had begun studying chimps in 1960 in East Africa. From that book, and eventually from her personally, I learned about the closeness of the genetic mix for chimpanzees vis-à-vis our human selves. I learned, too, how powerfully built they are—and how smart (including the ability to use makeshift tools to catch insects and crack nuts). Arnhem turned out to be special—with no animals in cages. In the same spirit of my increasing sense of what children really need, I was learning what animals deserve, too.

I said, "Yes."

Over the next two years, I raised $6.2 million. The Detroit Zoo's four-acre natural-habit chimpanzee exhibit opened in 1989. In the years since, millions have visited the exhibit called "The Great Apes of Harambee" (which means "Let's all pull together" in Swahili). Making that happen was a joy.

After that successful campaign, I was told multiple times, "If you can raise money for monkeys, you can raise it or anything." (Monkeys are, of course, primates, but not chimpanzees.)

Even more important to me than primates were, of course, people.

I emphasized getting as close to our readers as we could, and doing so without losing any integrity. To set an example, I—not a secretary—answered my own phone at every possible instance. Getting back to any caller the same day was fundamental to me, even if it were to say it would take a couple days to send a full answer. A quarter-century before, the

Free Press—led by the journalism giant Lee Hills—had billed itself as "The Friendly *Free Press*." That slogan was long out of use when I arrived in Detroit. But newspaper as "friend" rang true for me. A real friend really cares about you, even to telling you a "truth" you might not like. My approach to callers and readers was unusual enough that *The Wall Street Journal* wrote a front-page piece about editors, such as myself, working to get closer to readers. Already, newspapers, though before the time of the internet, were under considerable siege from other media, notably television. We clearly were not the only game in town. Distrust of the media (and other institutions) was growing, so much so that I led a task force on "credibility" for the American Society of Newspaper Editors.

As always, I was doing too much, working too much—born and raised unable to do things halfway. Even on "vacations," I answered phones and mail. I was never "off" even when I was off. Partly that's journalism; partly it's me. I've never known how to "relax"—and still don't.

At Tiger baseball games, I would mark corrections on page proofs (what the page would look like in print), but didn't miss any pitches. I brought work with me to my children's games and school productions, but never missed my own children when they were on the field or on stage. Lou Heldman, the *Free Press* business editor then, likes to tell the story of my bringing work to his wedding reception. Maybe I did, but I paid my respects to the bride and groom and chatted with every guest. As a motorist, I frightened passengers by speaking on early versions of portable phones and flipping through notes, all the while weaving in and out of traffic. Alvah H. Chapman Jr., the great leader of Knight Ridder, became so alarmed alongside me in the front seat that he ordered a driver for me. Once, doing a bit of editing at an antiques auction, with Bobbie alongside, I absentmindedly made the wrong gesture at the wrong time. We still have a $450 silver bowl that neither of us wanted.

Ben Burns, in my time the executive editor of the *Detroit News*, was quoted in that profile by Patty Edmonds: "Competing against Dave Lawrence is like competing against Darth Vader. He's just as fierce in his singleness of purpose."

Amidst all this, we had time for two more children—John and Dana, our fourth and fifth. Each furnished lessons for me that would lead me toward understanding what would be most important in my life.

John, our fourth child, had early hearing problems. For a while, it seemed he was deaf, but he outgrew whatever problem he had. Today he is married to Lacy—both now partners in Dallas law firms—and they have three beautiful daughters—Harper and the twins, Hanna and Rebecca.

Dana, born two decades after David III, is our youngest. She started school in Detroit, but was only four when we came to Miami. Dana, attending competitive schools that emphasized academics, did well for years. She is a wonderful writer and thinker—among the most compassionate, caring people I've known. She's the witty person in our family, knows how to make a point and be sensitive about it. I can never imagine her being hurtful to anyone. I remember her, age nine, accompanying me to the office one Saturday—always a good day for me to catch up and get ready for the week-to-be. For hours she sat patiently, watching TV with the volume turned down. Finally, she sketched something on a pad and handed it to me: "To Dad, Daddy, Father and Poppa: These are the things I *could* be doing! Reading. Playing a board game. Watching a movie. Eating."

I *can* take a hint. We left almost immediately.

But over the years there were signals—some we clearly didn't see at the time—that she wasn't especially happy. We didn't know anything was really wrong. At one point in her early elementary years, after our move to Miami, we did have to warn all of our children of serious death threats against me when I was publisher of the *Herald*. Our family cannot forget one Christmas Eve in 1992, when she was seven. We went to Mass that evening accompanied by two armed plainclothes police officers. Not until her adulthood did we find out how those times had affected Dana, who was convinced her parents were going to be killed. College didn't go well for her. We didn't know the problem; we did know she was depressed. Only in her late twenties was she finally diagnosed with ADD—often harder to detect in females. More recently, she was diagnosed with Complex PTSD (post-traumatic stress disorder), traced directly to those death threats. Now she is managing those challenges, and building a future. But had we known this many years earlier, she might have avoided so much pain.

Ultimately, as the newspaper war in Detroit raged, reality intruded. No one was going to take those losses forever. The newspaper business everywhere was beginning to falter—competition from other media, profit pressure from Wall Street, changes in American lifestyle, constant pressure from labor unions, and the beginning of automation throughout the newspaper.

Even though I didn't know it, Knight Ridder and the then-owners of the *News* were discussing the possibility of what was called a "joint operating agreement," known in the business as a JOA. Under the Newspaper Preservation Act, if you could prove that at least one of two newspapers in a city was "failing," those newspapers could combine business operations such as advertising, circulation, and production. So doing would eliminate duplicate functions and sharply reduce costs—while keeping the news and editorial pages separate, independent, and fully competitive (and thus, in this republic, preserve a vital voice). In 1985, Gannett, the biggest newspaper chain, bought the *News*. Discussions over the possibility of a JOA proceeded between the parent companies, though I was in the dark.

To achieve approval would require substantial pain for newspaper people concerned about their jobs and futures. There would be lengthy regulatory and legal hearings and long waits for rulings. Competitive people—and the best journalists are highly competitive—have no interest in playing for ties.

I had no interest in a JOA, but I wasn't making the decision. If this proceeded, I would need to manage two thousand people in deep uncertainty for maybe years. It was the most difficult assignment I ever had. How, for instance, do you keep the best people when it is quite possible you won't have a job for them one day?

In March of 1986 I learned about Knight Ridder's decision to go for a JOA. Not long after, it was revealed to staff and public that the *Free Press* would apply to the U.S. Department of Justice for JOA protection as a "failing newspaper." A "failing newspaper"? Nobody had "failed" on my watch. We had given everything we had, and were fully ready to give more and more.

But...

There was no other choice. My mission would become: Save the newspaper. Limit the human hurt. Preserve every job possible. Get this over as quickly as possible, and survive to thrive on producing high-quality journalism. We submitted reams of records and dumps of data. Testified in court hearings. Lobbied political, civic, business, and union leaders. Some employees despised any efforts to plead for a future. But it had to be done, and I had to lead that.

Two years of uncertainty followed. Then, on August 8, 1988, the Attorney General of the United States approved the JOA, followed swiftly by a court appeal that came from unions worried about losing jobs. The Supreme Court of the United States agreed to look at the case. More limbo. It was an excruciatingly painful wait.

I had known since 1987—though the staff did not know— that ultimately I would be going to Miami as publisher and chairman of the *Miami Herald* and *El Nuevo Herald*. Bobbie, the children, and I would have preferred to stay in Detroit. We loved it there. Two of our five children—John and Dana— were born there. I was deeply involved in the community as well as the newspaper. We had established real friendships. Moreover, who in one's right mind would want to work with the corporate headquarters one floor above the *Miami Herald* newsroom? Not I.

But that was the decision at Knight Ridder. I began to prepare myself, reading the *Herald* daily and taking Spanish lessons. (At our home in Grosse Pointe Park, Michigan, were Spanish-language labels on furniture and other household items and rooms.)

By this time, we were either going to get a favorable ruling from the Supreme Court, or the *Free Press* was gone. Those were the only options.

I had been determined to see it through, but Knight Ridder decided to bring me to Miami early because there was nothing more for me to do in Detroit. On July 27, 1989, I bid farewell to my staff at the *Free Press*. I was overcome with emotion. My going-away party was at Tiger Stadium; that afternoon we had access to every bleacher seat, the infield, the outfield, everything. (The JOA went ahead four months later via a 4-4 tie vote in the Supreme Court.)

By then, we were immersed in Miami.

A Life Lesson Learned:

Any prejudice we have, we learned. God did not give it to us. The best people struggle all our lives with the human tendency to feel most comfortable with people who seem like ourselves. The best people confront themselves. I often ask audiences, "Whom did you have in your home in the last six months?" It is telling.

---

*"When I say I want to photograph someone,
what it really means is that I'd like to know them."*
—American portrait photographer Annie Leibovitz

The pictures that follow tell some of the story—from the
earliest days in Manhattan to the farming years in upstate
New York and then to big newsrooms and beyond. Childhood
and children furnish the thread connecting my fabric of life.
The values I learned on that farm have buttressed all my
work, indeed my whole life.

David and Nancy Lawrence in New York City before the years on the farm.

David Lawrence Jr. at 8 months.

David and Nancy Lawrence—parents of nine—on the chicken farm in upstate New York.

Roberta and David Lawrence Jr. with their first-born, David III.

As executive editor of The Charlotte Observer *in the late Seventies.*

Roberta and David Lawrence Jr. on a park bench in Helsinki, Finland in 1984.

As publisher of the Detroit Free Press *in the Eighties.*

Testifying in court in 1987 on a proposed Joint Operating Agreement between the Detroit Free Press *and* Detroit News.

Going-away gathering at Tiger Stadium in 1989.

EⁱⁱR

The Master of the Household
is commanded by Her Majesty to invite

Mr and Mrs Lawrence

to a Dinner to be given by
The Queen and The Duke of Edinburgh
on board H.M. Yacht Britannia at Miami
on Friday, 17th May, 1991 at 7.30 p.m.

A reply is requested by 1st May, to:
H.M Consul, British Consulate
1001 South Bayshore Drive
Miami FL 33131-4936
Tel (305) 372-0270
Guests are asked to arrive between 6.50 and 7.05 p.m. at Terminal 12, Port of Miami   Dress: Black Tie

A 1991 invitation to dinner with Queen Elizabeth II.

Introducing President George H.W. Bush in 1992 before the American Society of Newspaper Editors.

With author Gabriel García Márquez in 1993.

With President Clinton on Air Force One in 1994.

Being introduced by Cardinal Keeler of Baltimore to Pope John Paul II in the late Nineties.

In an early learning center in Milwaukee, Wisconsin.

With Florida Governor Lawton Chiles, wife Roberta and daughter Amanda in the mid-1990s.

Helping son John, age 5, with his ice skates before a hockey game.

With Barack Obama as he campaigned for President.

At a black-tie function in Miami.

The Lawrences—including five children, a daughter-in-law, two sons-in-law, and seven grandchildren—at Disney World in the summer of 2017.

The most recent David Lawrence Jr.

CHAPTER 9
THE MESSAGES OF MIAMI

"In a way the world is a great liar. It shows you it worships and admires money, but at the end of the day it doesn't. It says it adores fame and celebrity, but it doesn't—not really. The world admires, and wants to hold onto, and not lose, goodness. It admires virtue. At the end it gives its greatest tributes to generosity, honesty, courage, mercy, talents well used, talents that—brought into the world—make it better. That's what we talk about in eulogies, because that's what's important. We don't say, 'The thing about Joe was he was rich.' We say, if we can, 'The thing about Joe was he took care of people.'"

—*Wall Street Journal* columnist and ex-presidential speechwriter Peggy Noonan

When I came to Miami in 1989 to run the *Herald* and *El Nuevo Herald*, the first words of advice came from the community's most significant figure for most of a half-century. That was Alvah Chapman, leader of death-defying B-17 bombing missions in his early twenties over Europe in World War II, the top civic leader in South Florida, the epitome of Old Testament Biblical morality, able to reach Presidents at a single bound!—and the top executive at one of the century's greatest newspaper companies. He was also the most strong-willed executive I've ever known. If Alvah decided a wall over there needed to come down—and solely by telepathy—somehow, I am sure, it would collapse.

A business executive deeply committed to growing profits, he also saw his mission to protect the journalistic and human values of the newspapers. Alvah believed that newspapers were a business, but not only that. He was mindful that you could outsource a shoe factory, but not a newspaper. Either the *Herald* makes it in Miami, or it doesn't make it at all. A successful newspaper and a successful community go hand in hand, he believed. He never thought newspapering was about protecting "sacred cows"; he did think that good newspapering meant getting the facts, all of them, being fair, revealing wrongdoings, and being unafraid to celebrate good people and good things.

As I arrived in Miami, Alvah gave me a list of fifty people I should know. I asked each many questions, ending with, "Whom else should I meet?" I met those people, too. I read a half-dozen books on Miami, and four newspapers closely every day. My Spanish lessons continued, supplemented by several weeks with a tutor in Uruguay (a South American country small enough in population that English wasn't readily heard). As I did in Charlotte and Detroit, I insisted that top editors and managers get out of the office and into neighborhoods.

In my first months, I met with all twenty-six hundred *Herald* employees, many individually, and spent significant time over the following years in every single corner of the newspaper—pressroom to circulation to advertising, everywhere. In my first major speech to *Herald* people I said: "I hope you will come to say, 'He listens. He tries to be fair. He is even willing to change his mind sometimes. He cares about this newspaper, and he cares about me.' " I had three assistants (two who helped with letters and appointments) plus a driver (making it easier for me to read and make phone calls in the car). Readers used to the preventive shield of voicemail were startled to get me directly. Two or three times a year, I would hear from a reader so hateful and so crude that I would have to say, "Ma'am, I have decided you cannot take the paper anymore." (They never knew how to handle that.) I sought to set an example that every letter, every phone call, every email be answered the day it was received.

In those years, the *Herald* was a money machine—tens of millions of dollars in profit every year. We were known nationally for high-quality journalism, tough investigative reporting, innovation ("Business Monday" and "Neighbors" sections covering news closest to home). We were sometimes very good—and frequently pretty smug. When waves of Cubans arrived on our shores after Fidel Castro's successful revolution in 1959, the *Herald* had little idea of what was really happening. Its mindset: The "usual" immigrant story of American assimilation would play out, and English would soon be everyone's tongue. Meanwhile, most of those Cuban exiles—not "immigrants"—thought Fidel Castro would be gone soon. The Bay of Pigs proved otherwise. It took fifty-seven years after the revolution of 1959 for Fidel to die. Even then, no-better brother Raul was in charge.

Most in that first wave of exiles—even if they brought little or no money—came from families used to education and success. They were willing to take the most menial jobs—and frequently not just one job. They were eager to "get ahead," do well for themselves and their families, and many became extraordinary American success stories. In the decades that followed, newer waves of Cubans came from less-privileged socioeconomic backgrounds, but with a resourcefulness learned from enduring life in a corrupt dictatorship.

The *Herald* made its first foray in the early Sixties into Spanish-language journalism with some translated articles. That was followed by *El Miami Herald* in 1976, a translated version of the *Miami Herald*. The *Herald* still didn't "get it." Indeed, it took the *Herald* decades to find out that many of our potential Spanish-language customers wanted *their own* newspaper. That didn't happen until 1987, when *El Nuevo Herald* debuted with its own reporting and columnists.

Two years later, I arrived in Miami. *El Nuevo Herald*—under the superb leadership of Cuban American Roberto Suarez, with whom I had worked in Charlotte—had its own mission and momentum. The *Miami Herald*, meanwhile, oftentimes remained in denial of how the community was changing. The *Herald* was frequently doing superb journalism, much of it focused on corruption, but was frequently out of touch with a changing community. Winning a bundle of national journalism prizes—all the while making a bundle of money—made it hard to change. Change was threatening to many in the newsroom. The staff of the English-language *Herald* was far less diverse than it needed to be. I insisted on that changing, and it did.

The ultimate breakthrough for a most meaningful *El Nuevo Herald* came not long before I departed. It took my assent, but most of all it took the insistent leadership of Alberto Ibargüen, the paper's publisher. He knew—even more than I—that Spanish-language customers wanted their own newspaper, available to be sold separately from the *Miami Herald*. It turned out to be a good reader decision (meaning more readers) and a good business decision (meaning ad revenue increases). There would be newsprint cost savings, too, when a reader could buy *El Nuevo* and not be forced to buy the *Miami Herald* as well. To use Alberto's words, "You cannot build community without first fully respecting the folks you want to meld into the whole." Amen.

Life was never simple for either *Herald*. In the early Eighties, a few years before I arrived in Miami, Jorge Mas Canosa, a successful businessman, and others created the Cuban American National Foundation (CANF). It became a powerful conservative force in Miami and the single most powerful voice in Washington vis-à-vis U.S. policy toward Cuba.

Mas Canosa, like Castro, didn't much cotton to anyone who thought differently than he—most especially if it had anything to do with Cuba. He despised the newspaper quoting people who thought differently than he about Cuba. Anything that would smack of re-examining U.S.–Cuba policy—a policy that still hadn't led to freedom for the people of Cuba—was anathema to him. In my time as publisher, he escalated his attacks on the *Herald*. In 1992, he said this on the powerful medium of Spanish-language radio: "The *Miami Herald* takes and assumes the same positions as the Cuban government, but we must confess that once upon a time they were more discreet about it. Lately the distance between the *Miami Herald* and Fidel Castro has narrowed considerably.... Why must we consent to the *Miami Herald* and *El Nuevo Herald* continuing a destructive campaign full of hatred for the Cuban exile, when ultimately they live and eat, economically speaking, on our support. These attacks...aim to destroy the authentic and genuine values of the Cuban-American community."

"Increíble!" to use the Spanish word. A newspaper of credibility covers the news—all the news—and carries diverse opinions. Then readers make up their own minds. To say that we supported Castro's communist regime was hogwash. Castro, in fact, regularly attacked us in his speeches. The Cuban government refused to give visas to our reporters; we had to sneak in and out of Cuba as "tourists" to cover anything on the island and depend on dissidents on the island to tell us what was going on.

But it was nothing to dismiss casually. Indeed, it became deadly serious. The foundation launched a boycott of both newspapers. Bus benches and bus signs carried "I DON'T BELIEVE THE *HERALD*" and "YO NO CREO EL *HERALD*." Newspaper vending machines were smeared with feces. (I accuse Jorge Mas of nothing, except stirring up some crazies.) The FBI came to me, saying the death threats to me personally were serious. Bobbie and I started our cars by remote control for two and a half years. We, of course, had to warn our children about all this—one of whom, Dana, was traumatized. At corporate headquarters, Jim Batten enhanced the security of our building, housing both *Herald–El Nuevo Herald* and Knight Ridder operations. Some of our employees found themselves caught between loyalty to the place they worked and pressures from relatives and neighbors.

As much as I remember the pain of that time. I also remember those in the Cuban-American community who rose to our defense. One was Dennis Pastrana, the highly respected president of Goodwill Industries of South Florida. In the Sixties, he had been a CIA agent who was infiltrated into Cuba for undercover operations intended to undermine the Castro regime. In a long letter that we published on a Sunday, our biggest circulation day, he wrote: "I thank you...for taking a stand on what is right and just, as difficult as this may be for you. You have made a significant contribution to the Cuban cause by flushing out the mentality and ideas about freedom from people who aspire to be the future leaders of the Cuban government and institutions. I can assure you that there are many Cubans who are grateful, and are taking notes."

Ultimately, Mas Canosa and the CANF quietly, and without notice, abandoned the campaign. Life went on, bumpy at times. The *Herald* needed to get better at understanding, better in portraying the depth and breadth of the community, and we did. Many in the Cuban-American community came to better understand us and our role. Tens upon tens of thousands of Cuban Americans became loyal *Herald* subscribers.

The Cuban-American community was important and deserved meaningful, thoughtful coverage, and commentary; so, too, did all the other communities we served in this, the least boring place in America, where the only constant is change. Miami, incorporated just four years before the turn of the twentieth century, is a community of stark contrasts—plutocratic wealth close by grating poverty.

Today, Greater Miami perches on the cutting edge of American pluralism. People like me—that is, non-Hispanic whites—are just 15 percent of the population, and only 12 percent of the thirty-five thousand babies born each year. Two-thirds of Miami-Dade's 2.8 million people (a population larger than sixteen states) are Hispanic; half of those are Cuban, with huge populations of Nicaraguans, Colombians, Dominicans, et al. For many in Miami, "black" and "African American" are not interchangeable terms; tens of thousands of people from Haiti and Jamaica and elsewhere identify as black or Afro-Caribbean but not necessarily as African American, and may, for one example, look at the matter of racism some differently. More than half of those in our community were born in another country. More than 60 percent of us speak a language other than English at home. (Tens upon tens of thousands of families want their children to hold onto their native language, knowing that that their children will be fluent English speakers in school.)

Culture is one of our many challenges. Different countries, different experiences, different governments. Democracy is in my DNA, and my growing-up years were spent in classrooms where portraits of Washington and Lincoln were hung above the blackboard. But that is not the story of Brazil, Colombia, Cuba, Haiti, Nicaragua and so many places from where

Miamians come. Steeped in the classic "American" story of immigration and assimilation, I had to unlearn some of what I thought was a given. I came to learn, for example, that those who came in the early years from Cuba saw themselves as "exiles" forced from their country—and not "immigrants." Assimilating and quickly losing one language to take on another would not be the course taken for many. For decades, hundreds of thousands held out hope to return to a free Cuba; it still hasn't happened.

My Miami is "American" to its core, previewing a not faraway moment when what we in these United States call "minorities" will be in the majority. In this giant "small town" of Greater Miami, a newcomer can quickly be involved in almost anything. (I was leading the countywide United Way campaign in my first years here; that would not have happened anywhere near that soon in any of the other six communities we have lived.) Miami has the capacity to show the rest of the country how to learn about one another, how to respect differences, how to celebrate what we have in common.

Miami, a gateway to the Americas, and connected everywhere in the world beyond, necessitates a newspaper with an appetite to understand every corner of the community and the more than a half-billion people who live below us in this hemisphere. That requires a staff with a great range of skills and perspectives. We needed to broaden and deepen our coverage, and not just of those of different national origins. As one example, we were among the first newspapers in the country with serious coverage of the gay community. We needed to write about good things and good people, giving readers a sense of who's working, what's working, who's giving. Everyone needs "role models." Any emphasis on so-called "good news" was bad news to some newsroom people. They thought it showed weakness; I thought it showed strength. The *Miami Herald* of those times was a proud and mighty battleship, and a battleship is hard to turn around. But we simply had to do some things differently, and better, without losing what made us strong and special.

As publisher, I was ultimately responsible for news coverage, the editorial pages, and all the "business-side" departments, including advertising, circulation and production. I wrote a Sunday column that focused on real people and shared values. Outside One Herald Plaza, I was deeply involved in the community and beyond. The *Herald*'s International edition was sold throughout the Caribbean and Latin America, giving me the opportunity to visit every country in the hemisphere. I interviewed many heads of state, among them Fidel Castro. The interview took place in Havana, in 1998, with other American editors and publishers. I asked the second question, which took him fifty-five minutes to answer. The dictator, then age seventy-two, clearly was "showing off"—both in the detail of his responses and his stamina over the five and a half hours of interview. (Afterwards, Castro signed a book for me, noting in pen the time he signed it—exactly 4:44 p.m. Only a man smitten with himself would do that.)

My journalistic travels included a boat ride on the Amazon where black and brown waters meet, and a ride in an open-door Soviet-built helicopter over the coca-growing fields of Peru's Upper Huallaga Valley. During these years my journalism colleagues elected me president of both the American Society of Newspaper Editors and the Inter American Press Association.

I led the local arrangements for the Summit of the Americas in 1994 where, hosted by President Clinton, every democratically elected head of state gathered in Miami. On the way to the summit from Washington, D.C., I interviewed President Clinton on Air Force One. Over the years I met him many times; this time we focused on the forthcoming summit. The treat on this occasion was traveling on the plane—splendid in space and furnishings. I came away with a good interview and presidentially labeled M&Ms for our children. With my wife as well as Jean and Jim Batten, we had dinner with Queen Elizabeth II. (Roberta curtsied and I bowed, and the Queen didn't say anything either of us can remember; Prince Philip wanted me to know that he admired the *Miami Herald*.) Jim and I were on the South Lawn of the White House when Yitzhak

Rabin and Yasser Arafat signed the Israeli–Palestinian peace agreement in 1993. Bobbie and I attended two State Dinners at the White House. In the course of my life and career, I have spoken with everyone who became President—from Nixon through Trump.

Certainly, I wouldn't have been able to do so many interesting things if not for the fact that I worked hard for powerful newspapers.

On a visit to Haiti, I dined with the U.S. ambassador, William Lacy Swing, one of our country's premier diplomats. The guests included Haitian President René Préval and his tourism minister, Maryse Pénette-Kedar. The dinner-table discussion centered around the state of education in that poorest country in the hemisphere. "If you get back to me with what area of education might make the most difference for Haiti," I said, "I'll see if there might be some way I could help." Two months later I was told: Vocational-technical education was the wisest way to go. Haiti is a country with too few skilled people, I heard; trained workers frequently must be hired from Jamaica and elsewhere to fill the needs of Haitian businesses. Returning to Haiti with my friend, Monsignor Franklyn Casale, the president of St. Thomas University, we visited vocational centers in Port-au-Prince. All were using outdated teaching tools and equipment. It would be tough to fix a late-model car, for instance, if your training had been on automobiles from the Fifties. With the aid of an interpreter, we talked with students whose principal ambition was to come to South Florida. That, of course, was not a recipe for "nation-building."

The Monsignor and I formed a compact with Haiti's Business–Industry Council, knowing that school wouldn't make much sense if its graduates couldn't get jobs. We formed a board, and made sure that the majority on that board were Haitian. Over the years, we came to work with quite extraordinary Haitians, among them siblings and business leaders such as Ralph Auguste and Michaëlle Auguste Saint-Natus.

The Monsignor and I went back home and raised a million dollars from South Floridians with a giving spirit, among them

Wini and Joe Amaturo, Peter Dolara and American Airlines, and Jan and Jim Moran and daughter Pat. There also was the generosity of Emilio Martinez, the patriarch of a large Miami homebuilding family. A Cuban exile, Emilio Martinez had never been to Haiti. With the Monsignor and me present, he gathered most of his nine children. "We need to remember what is truly important in this world," this father said to his children. "We need to remember that while our family had to start all over in this country, we were fortunate enough to be successful, and fortunate enough to be in this country where it is so possible. We need to remember how important it is to give back, to give to others." A few days later came a letter, a significant contribution, and this message: "Our help will be going where it is needed, the lowest level of poverty...and in a long-lasting way. Every member of our family will contribute to the extent of his or her ability." Giving us a further hand, the United States Southern Command, departing Haiti, turned over its thirty-thousand-square-foot headquarters near the Port-au-Prince International Airport to be used as the school.

Then came the day of dedication, September 11, 2001. We had arrived the previous day with a South Florida delegation of fifteen, including the funders. That morning, hell in the form of terrorism from the sky hit America. No planes would be flying for some time, meaning we would not be home for days. We spent that first morning watching it all on CNN, taking time out to dedicate what was called "Haiti Tec." The Monsignor said prayers for the enterprise and for Haiti and America. (I was a world away from Miami, and especially worried about our oldest son, the attorney who worked near the World Trade Center in New York City, and two college students at Georgetown University, not far from the Pentagon.)

In the years since, thousands of young Haitians have been trained and graduated in specialties including computers, construction, electronics, and air conditioning. The school is affordable for anyone who wants to learn and work. That *is* nation-building.

Nation-building occurs at home, too. In those same years, I came to know Joe Handleman, a fellow in his late eighties who had made his fortune in the sales and distribution business and used that wealth to help good causes in this country and in Israel. Our regular lunch meetings were personal and philosophical. This was a man of genuine wisdom.

At the same time, I also had met Father Jose Luis Menendez, the pastor of Corpus Christi Catholic Church and its accompanying parochial school in the Allapattah neighborhood of Miami-Dade. "Come visit the school," he said. "I want to show you something." What I saw was a school cafeteria in deplorable shape, paint peeling in sheets. No child should be eating there, I agreed. If several hundred thousand dollars could be raised, said Father, the children could have a "cafetorium"—a combination cafeteria and auditorium. "Could you help?" he asked.

Being almost genetically unable to say, "No," I raised those dollars. The biggest contribution—fifty thousand dollars—came from Joe Handleman. On the day of the celebratory dedication—in the cafetorium, of course—a beaming Father Jose Luis presided. The room was full of brown-faced children, most of them from the Dominican Republic, most still learning English. Accompanied by a guitar-playing nun, the children sang, in English, "God Bless America." The rest of us were all inspired. Hunched over in his walker—mind sharp, body frail, soul inspired—Joe leaned over and whispered to me, "Would you mind telling everyone that I will give another fifty thousand dollars?" "You need to do this, Joe." I said. "They need to hear from you." Haltingly, he moved toward the front and made his announcement. Father Jose Luis never had a bigger smile. The nun gasped. The children had no idea what was happening. We are at Corpus Christi (meaning "body of Christ"), and a Jewish man is affirming the best of humankind.

Once more, I was affirmed in my idealism and optimism.

So many generous people have supported my work with children. These and so many more: Cesar Alvarez, Tony Argiz, Jo Ann Bass, Trish and Dan Bell, Jerry Blair, Elaine and Phil Bloom, Ron Book, Paul Cejas, Betty Chapman and Dale Webb, Sue and Chuck Cobb, Armando Codina, Bill de la Sierra, Peter

Dolara, Lori Ferrell, Marshall Field V, Stuart Grossman, Debi and Larry Hoffman, Wayne Huizenga, Tina Hills, Sherrill Hudson, Alberto Ibargüen, Paul Tudor Jones, Hal Kaplan, Jonathan Katcher, Delores and Allen Lastinger, Jerry Lindzon, Charlie and Raul Martinez, Guillermo Martinez, Yusneli and Guimel Martinez, Melissa and Manny Medina, Gail Meyers and Andy Hall, Jeffrey and Stuart Miller and Leslie Miller Saiontz, Domingo Moreira, Mario Murgado, Nedra and Mark Oren, Jorge Perez, Neal Roth, Ron Sachs, Rafo Saldana, Debby and Jerry Schwartz, Pat Seitz and Alan Greer, Pat Snyder and Bob Crow, Jean and Bill Soman, H. T. Smith, Nadine and Tom van Straaten, Carol and Ed Williamson, Harriet Wolf, Juan Wong, and Richard Yulman. The list goes on and on. But one should not need riches to be remembered. In the Nineties I raised the dollars to keep open a Catholic school, St. Francis Xavier, serving mostly black children. Rose and Joe Munlin gave five dollars from Joe's tiny railroad pension. I have not forgotten them.

Connections are crucial to raising money. People believe in people. People give to people.

My computerized and every-day-added-to "Rolodex" contains more than fifteen thousand names accompanied by cell and home phones (office phone numbers aren't worth much anymore), home addresses, and email addresses. Most every day I meet someone new. I am my father's child, wanting to know everyone I can. I make myself available to anyone. Most mornings I have breakfast at a local bagel shop whose most interesting adornment is a blown-up 1938 police mugshot of Frank Sinatra. My "agenda" might be to discuss a community project, or maybe to help someone find a job and a next chapter in life, or help someone with a personal problem, or maybe to discuss a book. This is not about "cultivating" fund-raising prospects, but rather about learning from people and helping when I can.

Some of my greatest joys have come through journalism—due to the difference superb newspapering can make. Sometimes that wins Pulitzers; other times, the results arrive in ways less known but no less vital.

There was the time, in the mid-Nineties, when Virgilio and
Teresita Valdes came to me in deep agony. A year and a half
before, their son Danny had been murdered, and no one had
yet been arrested. Mr. and Mrs. Valdes had come to Miami
from Cuba in the mid-Sixties with three young sons to start
over. Could I do something so their son could be remembered?
I wrote a Sunday column about Danny Valdes, the victim.
His childhood. His First Communion. The dog he loved. The
books he read. The music he liked. His high school years,
then the architecture degree from the University of Miami. A
blossoming career in design. Then, his murder—shot six times
for his watch, his car phone, the cash in his wallet. A reader,
a woman who knew something about that murder, saw that
column. Months before, she wanted to go to the police, but her
family urged her not to "get involved." Now, remorseful and
conscience-stricken, she went to the police. That led to three
men being convicted of murder. In the interim, Mr. Valdes
had died of cancer. Danny's mother did have some closure,
though no real peace. "Your writing," she wrote me, "was the
cornerstone that permitted some justice."

What greater reason could there be for a journalist's life?

The best moments of my newspaper career came when the
journalism we did made the most difference. Hurricane
Andrew stands out. At that time the most costly storm in
the history of the United States, Andrew arrived in the early
morning hours of August 24, 1992. This beast of a Category 5
hurricane carried winds of up to 175 miles per hour, enough to
obliterate homes and neighborhoods.

In the space of six hours of darkness, we went from subtropical
paradise to pounding and peril. Andrew affected all of us
personally at the paper, but we still had to do our jobs. For
hundreds of thousands of residents, no power meant no
TV and, for some, no radio. There was no internet to access
for information. Where to find food and water and ice and
medical care? And, soon after, insurance adjusters? And law
enforcement? Many businesses were closed; advertising would
be sparse for weeks. Nonetheless, and appropriately, we spent
bundles of extra dollars on newsprint to give us more space to

tell stories. Overtime was a big expense. We did what was right to do. It was no time to think about profits. For a devastated community, the *Herald* delivered useful news and hope.

Never in my thirty-five years of newspapering was what we did more necessary. Only the *Herald* and *El Nuevo Herald* could really tell people what was happening, and how people could get help. And we did.

We helped many at the *Herald* itself, providing them with necessities and shelter. We didn't miss a day of publication. Led by Executive Editor Doug Clifton, we told the story of what had happened and what was happening. We gave practical advice about how to cope and where to find help. When help was slow to arrive, we sounded the call. Breaking with some professional precedent on the ethos of "objectivity," we used our front page to make the case: "We Need Help" read the most telling banner headline.

Distribution trucks and other vehicles were in short supply, but we found some. Fuel was hard to find, but we found some. Carriers were in short supply, so we delivered the papers ourselves.

Literally.

Many of our top editors and department heads and Knight Ridder's then-CEO, Jim Batten—and I and daughter Amanda, then sixteen—rode in the back of vans and pickup trucks and tossed papers on the lawn or driveway of every dwelling that seemed still occupied. We spent no time figuring out whether a subscriber lived there, or not. Everyone received the paper. That was our predawn duty for a month.

At the end, the *Miami Herald*—the entire staff, every one of us in every department, news-editorial and business-side— won the 1993 Pulitzer Prize Gold Medal for Public Service, the industry's top award. Said the citation: "For coverage that not only helped readers cope with Hurricane Andrew's devastation but also showed how lax zoning, inspection and building codes had contributed to the destruction."

It was one of five Pulitzers won by the *Herald* in my years there.

Every day is different in journalism. Some of those days could be rough. In the aftermath of Andrew, for example, thorough reporting and no-pussyfooting commentary led to an advertising boycott by Lennar, the giant homebuilder who had built some houses that didn't hold up in the storm. You hate to lose advertisers and money—we lost more than a half-million dollars in just this instance—but it happens. Even worse would be losing your journalistic soul, the sort of credibility and trustworthiness that provide a great home for advertising to sell homes and cars and more.

In the mid-Nineties, the economic engine began to sputter. In the shareholder-owned big public company that was Knight Ridder, there would be consequences. The competition from broadcast and print grew as people had ever more choices. Money-making had seemed as though it would go on forever. Then everything began to seem uphill. The internet was at the doorstep by the mid-Nineties, though we really had no idea of what a sweeping revolution it would bring.

In my decade at the *Herald*, we had a newsroom staff of more than four hundred. Ultimately, slowing profit growth and Knight Ridder targets forced us to begin layoffs. Most came from business divisions. The *Herald*'s newsroom staff never went below four hundred journalists throughout my decade there, though today the newsroom staff is a quarter of what it was when I departed in 1999.

Tough years passed. In early 1998, I was approached by Florida's attorney general and other powerful Democrats about running for governor. I—a lifelong newspaperman, compensated skeptic of politicians, and a registered Independent—was nonetheless intrigued.

From my teenage years, I thought of newspapering as a career in public service—and maybe someday, I thought even then, I might seek elected office. Being asked by serious folks to run for governor was a heady moment. Part of me said, "This is a job you could do. You care a lot about the issues. You would be able to help children, an issue in which you've become increasingly interested and involved. You know how to get people together. You are an inclusive person. You would be fair." So I took it seriously. Bobbie would have supported me, but my life for her already was plenty "public." Increased visibility wasn't her idea of what would be good for either of us. Moreover, we weren't "rich," and I did need a job. Running for office doesn't pay in any honorable, conventional sense, or shouldn't. And did I really want to spend much, if not most, of my waking hours raising money for myself? I turned down the opportunity, though I wondered subsequently whether I should have.

These restless times for me were accentuated by increasing pressures from the corporate folks one floor above my office at One Herald Plaza.

The paper still made good money. An 18 percent operating margin on almost $300 million in revenue is a mighty good business. But it wasn't enough for Knight Ridder, which decided that same year (1998) that we needed to increase that margin to 25 percent—or 25 cents operating profit on every dollar taken in—over the next three years. To be fair to Tony Ridder, the man who by then ran Knight Ridder, he wanted the company to be perceived as too strong to be taken over by another company. Tony had succeeded the legendary Jim Batten, who died tragically and way too young (age fifty-nine) from a brain tumor.

I told my bosses that I was getting too old, at age fifty-six, to lay off people, and wasn't sure I could live with myself if I did. I said we were now cutting into the very marrow of what makes the *Herald* and *El Nuevo Herald* most meaningful to our readers, that fewer journalists and others inevitably would mean diminished newspapers for our readers.

I was asked to see, before deciding, what it would take to get to that 25 percent. Department by department, *Herald* and *El Nuevo Herald* executives strategized about the math and the consequences. The bottom-line headline at which we arrived was this: We would have to lay off 185 more people.

(No business ever has found long-term survival by steadily diminishing its product and then asking an ever-decreasing number of customers to pay more for it.) How could I possibly live with that? I could not. But I did need a job.

I handle stress well, but despise uncertainty. What to do? Which way to turn? Then, while working in the office one Saturday morning in July 1998, the phone rang. Lee Hills was on the line. Then age ninety-two, he was among the twentieth century's greatest and most innovative newspaper leaders. Pulitzer winner. Right-hand man of Jack Knight, the patriarch of us all. Former publisher in both Detroit and Miami. First chairman of the combined Knight and Ridder. Guiding light of the John S. and James L. Knight Foundation. An exemplar of wisdom and rectitude.

"What's going on?" Mr. Hills asked, having no specific sense that anything was "going on." I hesitated. If you have reached ninety, I shouldn't be bothering you with my dilemmas. But for some reason I did tell him what was happening. "Jack Knight would be spinning in his grave," he said.

That seemed signal enough to me. I drove home to Coral Gables and spoke with Bobbie and son John, age eighteen and the only one of our five children at home that day. That weekend I wrote a resignation letter to my bosses:

> When you gave us the mandate for more profit several weeks ago, I told you that I would work hard to put together a plan that meets Knight Ridder's needs. Since then, we have made considerable progress in doing so while bearing in mind our first obligation to our readers and to the people who work here. But I also told you then that I would later let you know whether I, personally, could live with the results.
>
> In my 27 years in this company, with four newspapers as editor or publisher, I have spent a good amount of my time—especially these last two decades in Detroit and Miami—figuring what could be cut judiciously. In my nine years in Miami, we have reduced the payroll by almost 400 positions. (But I can say with some pride, the number of journalists here has increased slightly.)

Nonetheless, the toll on everyone has been great. To meet the bottom-line needs, we have done substantial slicing. Such measures as cutting back outstate circulation almost completely and spending nowhere near enough on promotion have been required to meet the short-term necessities, but have been a mistake long-term.

While I respect and recognize the realities of being a public company and what the shareholders might want and even insist upon, I also need to do what I think is right. And I do not think this is right.

I do believe that there is a strong future for newspapers of genuine excellence—newspapers that produce substantive coverage and commentary, newspapers with a depth of authoritativeness that no other medium can bring daily. And while I am confident that the plan we are putting together will do many good things and, on balance, we will be able to serve our readers well in both the Herald and El Nuevo Herald, I also strongly believe that first-rate newspapers require a greater, not diminished, commitment of resources.

The current process does have some good to say for it. It is always healthy to re-examine, especially in a business that serves an ever-changing readership. People here have accepted the challenge and are working hard to make sure we don't surrender any journalistic or human values and to improve these newspapers while cutting expenses. Nonetheless, I find myself weary of the cost-cutting over the years when, ultimately, I believe that we need to invest more....

That was that. Tony Ridder tried to talk me out of doing this, but my mind was made up. I made the resignation effective January 1, 1999, giving me five months to figure out a future.

I would be leaving the papers in good hands. Alberto Ibargüen, a trained lawyer and a principled leader, had been hired by me three years before from *Newsday* as publisher of *El Nuevo Herald*. He would be ably assisted by Joe Natoli, the president. Both were people who knew business and cared about journalism.

They would have to lead in a newspaper climate of rapidly accelerating change. Storm clouds already could be seen on the horizon, and the two *Heralds* already were scrambling for shelter. Where they landed would be on a fragile runway that offered no enduring protection. Many of our core readers were leaving the area or finding themselves working longer hours and having less time to peruse a newspaper. Many of them reached for other places to get news. Our core advertisers increasingly were finding productive alternatives to placing newspaper ads. Investors on Wall Street and elsewhere saw the same trends, and applied ever-intensifying pressure for profits. And the internet's seductive sun had dawned.

A front-page *Herald* story said only that I would be retiring the first of the coming year to spend my time in some area of public service and perhaps helping children, built from my service on a state taskforce looking at "school readiness." That wasn't much of a job description. I *did* need to work. I *did* need a paycheck. But as what to do now, I really didn't know.

I told just two people outside my family about my decision before it was announced. One was my closest friend, Dr. Pedro Jose Greer Jr., someone I love and trust totally. I also told another much loved friend, Jim Towey, once the legal counsel for Mother Teresa. "Now you're really going to find out who your friends are," he said. When you are a "big shot," everybody "likes" you, he reminded me. But what happens when you don't have power? I came to find out that if you have treated people decently when you have power, you will retain those relationships when you don't have power.

I was deluged by array of advice. One note arrived from the country's best-known advice columnist, Ann Landers: "Dear David Lawrence, Run for Gov. or the Senate. The next stop, the Presidency. We can use a guy like you. Cheers!"

While that made me feel good, I already had decided not to seek public office. I also didn't want to run another newspaper, having been managing editor or more of five daily newspapers over the previous twenty-nine years. Nor did I want to be dean of a journalism school—though twice asked; that would have been a life squeezed between faculty and administration.

Four days later, my clouds cleared.

Before telling that story, I share some final thoughts about journalism. Those thirty-five years in and around newsrooms turned out to be a vitally useful preface to my next chapter. What I had learned in journalism about fact-gathering, about storytelling, about leadership—all would be most necessary for what would turn out to be my most important chapter of life.

A Life Lesson Learned:

No one holds onto power and authority forever.
If you treat people well when you have power, you will have lifelong relationships, some quite helpful, when you no longer are "the boss."

CHAPTER 10

JOURNALISM: CRISIS AND CHALLENGE

"The point of modern propaganda isn't only to misinform or push an agenda. It is to exhaust your critical thinking, to annihilate truth."

—Chess grandmaster and Russian political activist Garry Kasparov

A profound new challenge confronts journalism—and the American people. It is an assault, supported by at least a third of American adults, on journalism and the very nature of truth. It is triggered and fueled by the most powerful person on the planet—the occupant of the Oval Office.

For me, the standards of journalism, the best journalism, ought never to change.

All my life, beginning with my parents, I've sought to exceed people's expectations. At the same time, I also have known that you cannot practice the most meaningful journalism and "please" all the time. Journalistic excellence requires coming across to readers, viewers, and listeners as someone who is genuinely fair. Most people know whether someone is really trying to be fair.

You'll not convince everyone, of course. A longtime *Herald* reader, Nicholas Burczyk of Lauderdale-by-the-Sea, regularly tested me. For years he would write me, never failing to indicate he was sending a copy to Pope John Paul II. Mr. Burczyk's central theme was this: "Holy Father, why do you tolerate the likes of Dave Lawrence running a newspaper?" One Christmas season Mr. Burczyk wanted the Pope to be aware of the *Herald* "paganizing" South Florida. Mr. Burczyk advised His Holiness to excommunicate me from the Holy Roman Church.

If you write me, you *will* hear back. My letter to Mr. Burczyk was quite brief: "Dear Mr. Burczyk: Someone under the influence of Satan has signed your name to a letter. You may want to get in touch with the police. This man is spewing and spreading hatred. God bless you." The archbishop and the Pope received indicated carbons.

Mostly, I heard from people less mean-spirited and more constructive—and frequently quite passionate.

My thirty-five years of everyday journalism frequently were exhilarating, often uplifting. That might mean the investigative piece that exposed stealing from the public, the illuminating profile of a community leader, the on-deadline scramble to cover a tragedy. Some days, some challenges led to exhaustion. It could have been brought about by a story way beneath my standards of fairness and genuinely hurtful to a human being who didn't deserve that. It could be the semi-incessant challenges of living within budget versus having the extra dollars to afford above-and-beyond journalism. Some days, I might go home wondering, "Why am I doing this?" But forever blessed by optimism and idealism, by the next morning my enthusiasm would be restored. The next day's opportunity— that is, every day in newspapering being different—is the beauty of the business.

In the Nineties, change accelerated for newspaper folks. While journalists cover change, most reporters and editors don't much like change themselves. While we generally thought of ourselves as in the "newspaper business," we actually were in the "news and information business"—assaulted by an increasing abundance of ferocious competitors. We were like those who thought they were in the train business (but actually in the transportation business), or the taxi business (blindsided by the convenience of Uber or Lyft), or in the bookstore business (to be pummeled by Amazon).

Two decades after "retirement," I still look at four newspapers a day—the *Miami Herald* and *The New York Times* home delivered, and *The Washington Post* and *The Wall Street Journal* online—plus at least two dozen pieces every day from websites (*Politico* being my favorite). People like me no longer set the media-consumption standard. Most young adults—and many older—now forego traditional newspapers. Home-delivery circulation has been ravaged, as has advertising revenue. Today, younger people mostly see a newspaper—if they do—online. Many of them click onto a story or two via an online app, and somehow convince themselves that they've "read" the newspaper that morning. Citizens of wisdom need to know what is going on. That's how we keep this republic. (To add to the challenges, most newspapers were foolishly slow to charge for online content.)

Competition for reader-viewer-listener attention is more ferocious than ever, and the media are more fragmented than ever. Thus far, all these extra choices have turned out not to have made us a more informed people. Attention spans have been eviscerated by 24/7 television "news," more sexy than serious. These days, most people seeking political news watch or read or listen to what fits their predilections and prejudices. Those truly informed receive their news and information from multiple sources—print to podcast—and then make up their own minds as to what they think. Minus genuinely informed and involved citizens—people who are interested in facts told in honest context—our republic is imperiled.

This isn't about "good" news vs. "bad" news. ("Good" and "bad" depend on the beholder.) Rather, it is about the increasing inability of citizens to get a full portrait of who's working and what's working in society. Today, most media energies—online or off-line—seem focused on serving titillating table scraps that fall to the floor of society rather than the meat and potatoes of information that, when fully digested, help citizens make the wisest decisions for community and country. Shame on us for buying it, reading it, listening to it, watching it, wallowing in it. Bleating and bluster so often prevail over serious journalism. But...

I remain an optimist. I do see serious efforts, including online, to produce serious journalism. In some ways, online gives us more good choices for good journalism than ever. My greatest worry is for local news, the news that hits closest to home. The decline of the traditional print newspaper means no longer are there large staffs devoted to basic coverage of the community. The *Miami Herald*, for instance, does pretty well considering the circumstances, having received more Pulitzers than any other newspaper in the Southeast. But no amount of purposeful energy can overcome the reality of a newsroom staff eviscerated by reality. Nothing ultimately is a "good-enough" substitute for a major-league newspaper, with a major-league staff, with page upon page devoted to everything from watchdog journalism to kid soccer scores.

Courtesy of the internet and a vast array of media, we have more choices than ever before. But who among us is taking the time to sample seriously, to reach out for not only the facts, but also conflicting perspectives?

How in the world did we get to this place?

A quarter-century ago, as president of the American Society of Newspaper Editors, I spoke to the annual convention about what I called "unsettling trends." Among these: Americans already were spending more time working and more time commuting, and had fewer paid days off. That left potential readers far less time to spend on what we were producing.

Meanwhile, more than twenty million U.S. adults were functionally illiterate. Ever-increasing numbers did not speak English as a first language—or at all. Even back then, up to half of all American registered voters didn't bother to vote. "That reflects a growing apathy, a lack of connectedness," I told my news-gathering colleagues. "People who do not feel bonded to communities are poor prospects for newspapers. Similarly, a bright future for newspapers absolutely depends on our ability to get close to everyday people and report what is truly meaningful to them. Journalistic detachment is vital, and it will be. Journalistic aloofness will be fatal. Newspapers may never again be a semi-automatic choice in readers' homes. That ought to make us tougher, wiser, and better. There are a great many things we can do to increase our chances of being chosen by readers."

I suggested that we rededicate ourselves to remaining relevant, devoting resources to our readers' concerns over the economy, the environment, and issues such as aging, career, urban development, and overdevelopment. Listen more closely to readers, I said; spend less time telling them why we can't do the stories they suggest, more time figuring out how to do those stories.

Sharing my devotion to diversity—racial, ethnic, gender and otherwise—I suggested that we "reflect our communities in our staffs, in our managements and on our pages. Diversity is the soul of what you and I are all about."

I also urged closer attention to customer service. "The fact of the matter is that we spend an extraordinary amount of money each year trying to get new readers—and perhaps we would be better off if we spent more of our energy and emphasis trying to keep the readers we already have," I said. "Every single encounter with readers, spoken or written, deserves a thoughtful and personal reply.... We need to be so very responsive that when people have dealings with us, even and sometimes especially so on those occasions when they are angry, they nonetheless feel compelled to acknowledge, 'At least they listen; they seem to be fair people; they seem to really care.' "

Prophetically, I warned about the hazards of blandness, urging my colleagues to guard each operation's individuality. "A newspaper's identity incorporates the nature of the local community and its local happenings, the columnists, the design, the layout, the historical roots, the practices and policies. Democracy absolutely cannot afford homogenized journalism. We ought to be democracy's greatest, most essential forum for vigorous debate, for the honorable confrontation of ideas and opinions. Instead, too often, we are simply bland. Newsrooms with aspirations of great excellence must have editors of great vision, and the enormous insistence to achieve that vision."

Twenty-five years later, those unsettling trends have intensified, leading to fewer people being adequately informed and no improvement in voting participation. Some negative trends, of course, could not have been predicted back then: competition from internet-based operations, utterly fake "news" (by which I mean actual fiction; I do not mean factual news that upsets a politician), politically tinged "news" that has ignited toxic political partisanship, plus politicians with little regard for truth and utter contempt for the media.

Newsrooms, while generally more diverse, also have become far thinner in staffing. This makes listening and responding to readers' news tips and concerns less likely. Newsroom people who remain tend to be younger and less experienced. Layoffs have denuded newsrooms of seasoned, experienced editors and administrators.

Bureau of Labor Statistics data for 2017, compiled by *Politico*, show daily and weekly newspaper publishers employed 175,000 reporters, editors, photographers, salespeople, etc. Impressed? Don't be. In 1990, 455,000 people were employed in those same roles. That's a hemorrhaging of 280,000 newspaper positions in just twenty-seven years—an average annual loss of more than ten thousand reporters, photographers, page designers, salespeople and others every single year.

All those positions added by internet publishers were not nearly enough to offset the losses in what we've come to call the "legacy media." In fact, today more people work in internet publishing than in newspapers. For any who might be reassured by this, know that it was newspapers that most avidly embraced traditional journalistic values and ambitions—qualities that have served our democracy well.

Add to that the tendency of national media outlets—newsrooms at our highest-quality newspapers and throughout the internet—to concentrate in urban, progressive population centers largely along both coasts. That means that news consumers in the vast majority of American communities are now underserved. In larger and, like it or not, more influential markets along the coasts, a growing majority of newsroom employees inevitably are influenced by the values and beliefs of those around whom they live and work. That means they can become increasingly out of touch with large numbers of their fellow Americans—those who live between the two coasts. The 2016 presidential election reminds us of all that.

At the same time, too many news people and their managers cling to a perverted sense of "fairness." Too often, they carry "both sides" of a story that, in reality, has only one side. In some cases this is because they are inexperienced and poorly trained; in other cases, it's because they are overworked and over-pressured to product quick-hit mini-stories. A full pursuit of the truth requires much more than quoting "two sides." Sometimes there is only one "side"; other times, many "sides." In the pursuit of fairness and real context, we are obliged to state "the truth" when we know it—and label a "lie" when it is. In the words of the late Senator Daniel Patrick Moynihan: "You are entitled to your opinion. But you are not entitled to your own facts."

A few news organizations, even as they confront financial restraints, remain aggressive. But many news organizations have descended into repositories of little meaning—the inevitable output of the homogenized journalism encouraged by profit-at-any-cost bosses. Too often today it's not about more staffing, tackling tough subjects, deep and readable (and sometimes entertaining) reports. More common are anemic, overmatched, under-managed staffs too often producing superficial, hyper-partisan stories that make no honest connection in readers' lives. Readers soon figure out they easily can do without such. In my day, mostly gone, I could judge newspapers on how much "unique" content they had— that is, what I can find in the *Herald* or *The Post* or *The Times* or wherever that can be found almost nowhere else. Take that test today, and you will find little that is really "unique."

Meanwhile, corporate leaders double-down on strategies that clearly have not worked. Once, twice, three times a year, every year, they further reduce staffs, further diminish the number of pages they print and further reduce the number of times they refresh their web pages, and increasingly dumb down their content, whether in print, on the internet or through broadcast. At the same time, instead of making substantive, positive changes, they descend deeper into managerial gibberish. They appoint "platform editors" and "audience engagement editors" and "storyteller editors" and so on. And they write robotic, consultant-influenced missives to their depressed, demoralized staffs. Here's one such memo from the editor of the besieged *Boston Globe*. Henceforth, he writes, his newspaper will be considered an "organization of interest." "We'll set up an Audience Engagement team," he tells his staff. "We will refine and refine again the Hub system that was proposed by the Mission working group."

Huh? What in the world are you talking about? How about just go out, find the news, and make it available in print or otherwise?

Journalism can be, and should be, a life of public service. A way to do good every single day. A way to make a daily difference in people's lives. A way to retain integrity, optimism, and idealism all one's life. A life of good and meaningful journalism is an exhilarating, challenging, never-dull life in a business that has constantly reinvented itself these past two centuries, and never more so than in recent years. It must continue to do so—all the while holding onto all the basic values of honesty, fairness, and getting as close to the truth as human beings can.

That should not change in any era. In the year 2000, a little more than a year after my transition to the world of early learning, I traveled to Sao Paulo, Brazil, to speak with young journalists there. Concerned by the continuing downward slide not only of our business prospects but also of our ambitions and our devotion to our craft, I felt compelled to remind them: "You have entered journalism, I trust and hope, not because you will be compensated in a certain monetary fashion, but because you will be compensated in your knowledge that you can shed light on the wrongs of society and shed light on the good people and good things in our midst, and in doing both will leave this world at least a bit better for other people."

We need that to be true. Forever.

Amidst all the serious and substantive moments of truth-seeking, my days frequently were laced with moments of humor. May I never forget *Detroit Free Press* reader Leo Bardach. Over the years he wrote often, his central theme being that he could never figure out why anyone so incompetent as I could possibly be in charge of a newspaper. One day, for instance, Mr. Bardach wrote: "Sitting in your ivory towers as you do every day, you are not aware of what is happening [to the newspaper.]... The [mistakes] are but a few examples of a circus and its clowns at work." As a simple matter of what I hope is decency, Mr. Bardach had at least one redeeming grace: He was ever the gentleman. So this letter ended: "Kindest regards." And here was Mr. Bardach, after a columnist won a journalism award: "Either the judges in the contest have never before read any of (his) columns, or they are boozies, flesh peddlers or hangers-on in bars and whorehouses, or are really stupid." Mr. Bardach ended this letter: "And a very pleasant day to you."

I would prefer to remember, of course, the moments of recognized achievement—the investigative series, for instance, that really make a difference—and the "small" moments of meaning to those of us who love this business.

I remember reader Dagoberto Oliva, who wanted me to know that the paper is "very kind to the voiceless." I remember what the newspaper meant to Andres Munera Ramirez, an oil worker deep inside Colombia, who sent me an email. He had just received, by helicopter, a copy of the *Miami Herald*. "We cannot leave [where we are] due to the guerrilla problems.... Just knowing about the world gives us something to comment about during the long nights."

The joy of a life is the difference that you make in other people's lives. In newspapering I found those opportunities every day.

So, where do we go from here?

First, nothing we do on our journalistic side of the transaction will make much difference if readers-viewers-listeners on the other side of the transaction cannot distinguish between real news and fake news or between truth and falsehoods. This inability to do so poses the gravest threat to American democracy of my lifetime. We are lost as a nation if we cannot trust the media to give us the whole story. The media are essential to the checks-and-balances of our republic. In the words of Thomas Jefferson, who had his own considerable conflicts with the press: "Were it left to me to decide whether we should have a government without newspapers or newspapers without a government, I should not hesitate a moment to prefer the latter."

To correct this, perhaps we need a national campaign called "Consider the Source." This public-service campaign would remind Americans to weigh carefully the credibility of the sources of their information—and help them do so.

We have no time to waste. Media credibility continues to erode. Yet despite the assault on the press, most Americans continue to believe that the news media have a vital role to play in keeping this republic. But, to quote the recent Gallup/Knight Foundation Survey on Trust, Media and Democracy, "most Americans believe it is now harder to be well-informed and to determine which news is accurate. They increasingly perceive the media as biased and struggle to identify objective news sources."

This challenge is not going away anytime soon—indeed, anytime. In today's world of packaged reality, when incivility is so fashionable, a news-gathering operation of the highest human and journalistic values is crucial. The basics still work—and always will. The criteria remain: Authoritative. Aggressive. Substantive. Thoughtful. Compassionate.

Interesting. Committed to reflecting the full community with words and with pictures. Trying to reach everyone. Helping a diverse people respect differences—and helping a diverse people understand what we have in common. Contributing to a real sense of *community*.

People want stories that are useful, that treat them seriously, that respect them and their interests. Journalism's future must focus on stories of real importance and tell them thoughtfully. (How, for instance, to understand the differences about Sunni and Shiite.) Journalism that tells the reader what is *really* going on. (What does "torture" mean, and where is it being employed—and should it be employed anywhere?) Journalism unafraid to celebrate good people and human achievement. (Not just profiles of the best known, but also lesser-known role models for us all.) Journalism unhesitant in its pursuit of wrongdoing. (The corruption in community and country.)

I see a future for journalism neither simplistic nor boosterish. Journalism as the clear-eyed friend, willing to criticize, unafraid to praise, urgent in a search for solutions. Journalism that understands the necessity of, and connection with, news operations in a democracy. Journalism that moves people to noble purpose. Journalism that embraces the fundamental values that shape a good life and a good community—truth-telling, fairness, caring, diversity, goodwill, and respect toward all. I do not speak of journalistic pablum, but I do see a hunger for telling stories that call out, and inspire, the best in each of us.

Nowhere is it written that newspapers or any medium have a divine right to a future. Yes, the challenge is difficult. Yes, the world has never changed this fast. Yes, we live in a world that is hurry-hurry-hurry—and could you speed up some more? Nothing lets up. Demographics are changing constantly. We are in the midst of an extraordinary cultural revolution.

I share a dozen imperatives for giving journalism and journalists a better chance at a bright future:

1. We must get more reporters out on the street. Editors, too. How much listening are we really doing? How well

do we really know the community? Most of us spend too much time with people too much like ourselves. This is not good for the best journalism. Corporate managers need to begin rebuilding resources. While other operations continued to cut into the bones of their operations, *The Washington Post*, re-energized by a new, deep-pocketed owner and an aggressive new editor, saw its profitability rebound to the point where it was able to add dozens of journalists to an already-muscular newsroom. *The New York Times*, still the best of American newspapers, has added hundreds of thousands of digital customers; it speaks to readers eager for serious journalism and genuine engagement. *The Wall Street Journal* has never been better.

2. We must have a diverse staff and management—reflective of the community in every possible way—to understand the community well enough to succeed.

3. Newspapers must "own" local content, the news that is closest to people's lives. This ought to be our basic strength. Too often it is not. I buy the *Miami Herald* for reasons that begin by telling me what is happening in my own community.

4. Good journalism must never be routine. A good part of journalism's future depends on story-tellers who soak up and share the detail, and who have the wisdom and skills to write stories of real context.

5. Journalists must be truly passionate about accuracy. Many people in this business are not. If you have ever been covered, as I have, then you know exactly what I mean.

6. We must push like hell to uncover wrongdoing anywhere it exists. "Watchdog journalism" is at the very heart of our obligation.

7. Speaking of "heart," we ought to be compassionate—and see that as a strength. Our real test is not our compassion for the downtrodden—most of us have

that—but whether we can be sensitive and thoughtful and fair to those with whom we disagree, those we instinctively might dislike. Journalists are not big-game hunters. Showing respect must be a strength.

8. We should stop being so risk-averse. Nowadays we are in peril of becoming an afterthought. A little tinkering is not genuine change. Real change means stories and illustrations that are markedly different, and better, than you can get anywhere else.

9. We ought not to be suckered into feeling sorry for ourselves that we missed some "golden era." It was never as good as we recall it. The day of the journalist as idealist need not be gone. Good journalism can always make its mark on our world.

10. Journalism's best path to the future is not "dumbing it down" in a mad drive to compete, but rather doing what is respectful of readers (and viewers and listeners). They should receive what they say they want, plus what really good editors know they will need—everything from authoritative stories that are necessary in their lives to children's T-ball scores—compelling reading on every level for which people will want to make the time.

11. Each of us must be really willing to learn. We need to be people who read good books regularly, beginning with history and biographies. Much can be learned from other lives.

12. We never should be embarrassed to write about good people and good things. The media share a responsibility for pervasive cynicism, apathy, and antipathy toward public institutions and public servants. Most of the world is not corrupt and sleazy. Most of the world is populated by decent people trying to do the best they can. We should write about them and the places they work. Done right, this is not "puffery." It is in-depth examination of institutions or programs or people who are doing their jobs. It is examining

taxation and spending to see what is justified, needed, and worthy—not just to find waste, though that is important, too. People want hope. Hopeful people become involved in public life. They will be consumers of good journalism.

On our watch, the freedoms of this country are in danger of being significantly and tragically eroded. I fear for the future of this country if we go timid in a time of terrorism—and political antagonism. The newspaper as watchdog is at the heart of our obligations in this republic. In the decades-ago wisdom of Justice Louis Brandeis: "The greatest menace to freedom is an inert people." Said the Rev. Dr. Martin Luther King Jr.: "To accept passively an unjust system is to cooperate with that system; thereby the oppressed becomes as evil as the oppressor. Non-cooperation with evil is as much a moral obligation as is cooperation with good."

I hope for a future where generations to come will enter this business for the same reasons I did—for ideals of public service and the honorable desire to make this world better.

While too many in media focus on instant gratification, news operations of genuine excellence can provide the coverage and commentary that prod people to think for themselves. Democracy thrives on reflection. Democracy needs journalism as the watchdog of the public purse and the public good.

We have so much to do, and need to do it now, accompanied by all the honest purposefulness that we can muster.

Our very republic is at stake.

A Life Lesson Learned:

Most people are neither corrupt nor sleazy. Most people are decent, seeking to lead meaningful lives that make a difference. People deserve to be recognized and celebrated long before a funeral service. We all need "role models."

CHAPTER 11
COULD I EVEN DO THIS?

"I frankly yearn for the opportunity to decide what I want to do with my life,"
Lawrence told hundreds of reporters, editors, salespeople, production workers
and support staff gathered in the company's cafeteria.... His announcement
produced stunned disbelief. After he spoke, the staff showered him with
45 seconds of applause and a standing ovation. Lawrence dissolved
into tears, as did some employees."

–From the *Miami Herald*, August 5, 1999

That front-page *Herald* story said I would retire in five months
and wanted some time to figure out a next chapter that *might*
involve public service and early childhood education.

There you have it: Something to do with children. Something
to do with public service. Not exactly a full description of a
next chapter of life and work.

But it was enough for one man reading the story—Gerald
Katcher, resident of Miami most of the year, summer home in
Aspen, Colorado. From the latter, twenty-two hundred miles
away, came the phone call that made my next chapter possible.

Jerry Katcher was still running a bank he had grown from one
branch to many and that he had sold to Mellon in Pittsburgh;
his wife Jane is a retired medical doctor. Three of our children
went to the same school as their children. We knew the family,
but were not then close friends.

They had been at our home. In the Nineties, Bobbie and I
hosted every-other-year Christmas–Chanukah gatherings in
our backyard. We'd invite one hundred and fifty or so people
for hors d'oeuvres and drinks and conversation. One year the
guest list—meeting every test of diversity—included a United

States senator, the archbishop, and a fellow who had served time for anti-Castro violence in the United States. The guests ranged from the well-known to those known only to me. The next day Jerry, one of those guests, called me to say, "I was struck by all the different people you had there yesterday. I am on the board of the New World Symphony, and we are always talking about more diversity. Can you send me some ideas for potential board members?" The next day I sent him fifty names, addresses, and phone numbers. He never forgot the range of people or the alacrity of my response. He also admired my weekly *Herald* column that focused on people and principles and building "community."

So when it was announced that I would be retiring the following January, he called from Aspen the end of that week to say, "We do not want you to leave Miami. You are important to Jane and me and to our community. If you want to stay here and work on children's issues, I will set up a foundation."

I could not have imagined this. His call did not erase my doubts. Indeed, I was beset by doubts. "Are you sure, Jerry?" I asked. "I believe in you," he said. "That is enough." That he and Jane believed in me so deeply—would be so willing to take such a chance—was as great a gift as I could be given. If not for the Katchers, we probably would have been living someplace else and doing who knows what.

The Katchers gave me a runway for the future. But what sort of plane would I pilot? And where was I going?

I did not yet know enough to know what could make a difference in children's lives and futures. From my two years of civic service in the mid-Nineties chairing the Readiness Committee on the Governor's Commission on Education, I had learned that if we could ever get the first few years right—the time when most brain growth occurs—far more children would succeed in school and in life. If I have a special strength, it is as a dedicated, even driven learner. Already, I had read a lot, asked a ton of questions, and traveled to so many child care and early childhood centers—like the one I would later visit in Liberty City. But I certainly didn't know anywhere near enough.

It would take many "Old MacDonald" sorts of stories for me to be on firm ground as to what constituted "quality" and how crucial it was to positive outcomes for children.

I was running scared. And that is good: It makes me run faster, harder—and learn more.

I only knew two things for sure: (1) early learning is crucial, and (2) how little I knew.

What difference could I really make? What needed to be done? How could I help make that happen?

My learning had started at home. There I could know that a loving, knowledgeable, caring parent—Roberta, for example— was vital in our five children turning out to be good adults. There I could remember our own experience in reading with our children, taking them to interesting places (from jails to evangelical tent festivals), meeting the high and mighty *and* the impoverished, the powerful and the powerless. From their childhoods I could see how the high-quality Montessori centers each attended made a difference not only in their early literacy abilities, but also in how well they connected and played with other children, how good they felt about themselves.

Much of my life's lessons came from reading—not only of newspapers to know what is going on in the world around us, but also of books, especially history and biographies. There was much to be learned from history, and much to be learned from the lives of great men and women—what they achieved, where they fell short. Enduring change is difficult to do. Half a millennium ago, Niccolo Machiavelli told us in "The Prince":

> *There is nothing more difficult to take in hand, more perilous to conduct, or more uncertain in its success, than to take the lead in the introduction of a new order of things. For the reformer has enemies in all those who profit by the old order, and only lukewarm defenders in all those who would profit by the new order, this lukewarmness arising partly from fear of their adversaries...and partly from the incredulity of mankind, who do not truly believe in anything new until they have had actual experience of it.*

My reading of history has reminded me that all social progress in history has been preceded by pushing and shoving. The great American Frederick Douglass told us: "Power concedes nothing without a demand; it never has, and it never will." How to apply all this to my own next chapter? How would I push—politely when possible?

Turning the opening pages of that next chapter, I traveled to Europe to see firsthand how some nations—France being the best example—make high-quality early childhood settings available for *every* child. Could we do that in my own community? Could my own community serve as a good example of what could be done in my own country?

To learn and come to understand, I ask question after question, then at least one more. Many of those questions are personal—about your family, what you read, what you watch. Ask enough good questions, a full portrait begins to emerge. My questioning began in my own community and in my own state, then segued elsewhere in my own country; I traveled to the likes of Atlanta, Georgia; New Haven, Connecticut; Independence Missouri; and Washington, D.C. Then I went to France, Sweden, and Italy—all countries significantly advanced beyond our own in getting children off to a brain-stimulating start in the crucial first five years of life. (While the great power in health and education in most of the rest of the world is to be found in each nation's capital, in the United States it is a *local* power. It is, by way of example, the 2.8 million people of Miami-Dade County deciding what *they* want for *their* children.)

Educated by observation and experts as well as the lessons of history, I came to conclude this: My mission would embrace *everyone's* child. It could never be about *those* children, whomever they might be, however justified it might seem. It would have to be about *our* children, *all* our children, with the understanding that *all* children need the basics of health and education and knowledgeable nurturing.

But how to do that? What would that really mean? Would people, many of whom knew far more than I about the subject, listen to me? (If I heretofore seemed *powerful* to some people,

I no longer was.) Would I listen to them? Would I be a good learner? How could I earn their trust?

What—specifically—should I take on? What would be real progress for children? How would "progress" be measured?

What could I—the journalist and newspaper publisher— bring to the table? I had some strengths: I knew people in every corner of the community. I had been part of my state beginning when I was fourteen years old. I knew people of means and power and money, and had raised dollars for high causes. I had an appetite and aptitude for convening and collaborating. I was used to writing and public speaking. I was not discomfited by people knowing more than I on a topic because I could surround myself with knowledgeable people. I loved to learn (and I had so much to learn). Already, I knew enough to believe in the cause. Indeed, I came to think "school readiness" spoke to the future of America, including its national security.

All these reasons made sense. I was still nervous. Very. Could I really make any real difference for children? My next and most meaningful chapter did not start as a *sure thing*.

A Life Lesson Learned:

I like to be nervous in embarking on almost anything—giving a speech, shepherding a project, running a meeting. It makes me run harder and faster, think more deeply, work harder to connect.

CHAPTER 12

DEVOTING THE REST OF MY LIFE TO CHILDREN— *ALL* CHILDREN

"Once you are interested in shaping children's lives, you will never be interested in anything else again. There is nothing greater."

—Legendary dancer Isadora Duncan

One of a publisher's roles is as civic leader, responsible for one of the community's most significant enterprises and whose mission is to tell readers and citizens every single day what is going on—good and bad—and how things might be made better. Under that mantle, I agreed to serve on Governor Chiles's commission with its charge to make recommendations on how to educate Floridians for the forthcoming millennium. As for my assigned responsibilities of "school readiness," I knew precious little. What I came to learn preceded, and catalyzed, my most important passage in life.

Our children—David III, Jennifer, Amanda, John, and Dana— were raised according to the principles of what I years later understood as high-quality early childhood care, development, and education, even if I had not heretofore known those were "principles." *Every* child, I came to understand, needs what our five children received—a blend of health and education and nurturing and love.

I traveled to places like France with its early childhood quality-for-everyone approach called *école maternelle*, and to Italy with its child-centered Reggio Emilia centers, and across these United States to witness the best advances in early learning. I met with experts, and read extensively. There was, for instance, the 1999 book by Alison Gopnik, Andrew Meltzoff, and Patricia Kuhl. In that book, *The Scientist in the Crib: Minds, Brains and How Children Learn*, I read this:

> *Walk upstairs, open the door gently, and look in the crib. What do you see? Most of us see a picture of innocence and helplessness, a clean slate. But, in fact, what we see in the crib is the greatest mind that has ever existed, the most powerful learning machine in the universe. The tiny fingers and mouth are exploration devices that probe the alien world around them with more precision than any Mars Rover. The crumpled ears take a buzz of incomprehensible noise and flawlessly turn it into meaningful language. The wide eyes that sometimes seem to peer into your very soul actually do just that, deciphering your deepest feelings. The downy head surrounds a brain that is forming millions of new connections every day.*

Back then, the matter of brain research had never crossed my mind. But I came to know about the "explosion of learning" that occurs right after birth. I came to know about the trillions of connections between neurons, a number that diminishes as connections are never used. I came to know why I will never speak Spanish perfectly, no matter how hard I continue to try, but how different it might have been had I the abundance of cerebral synapses that were mine seven decades ago.

What I learned gave my life newly energized purposefulness.

Thus, with the newspaper business now requiring more energy to figure out what to subtract (beginning with staff) rather than what to add, I "retired." It was a risky move. To use a double negative, I could not afford not to have a job paying real money. We had colleges to pay for, and a home, and all the usual bills. I was willing to make less. (Much less, it turned out.) Roberta could not have been more understanding.

After making my retirement announcement and getting that call from the Katchers, a next chapter seemed more real. What Jane and Jerry Katcher made possible was The Early Childhood Initiative Foundation—what years later became The Children's Movement of Florida. Between the Katchers' generosity, and that of another Miami-based couple, Jan and

Dan Lewis, we had enough money to get started on doing something important on behalf of children. I would need to raise many more dollars to do the work, but their generosity meant we could launch our work with a small staff.

I had spent thirty-five years in the storytelling business of journalism. But so much of my energy, and that of my colleagues, had been spent on stories that told what had gone terribly wrong in our society. Never enough energy was used in what would make things better. Now would be the time to tell different stories—ones that could lead to better futures for children. All my life—going back to selling vegetables at the age of ten—I have been a salesman of sorts. For this next life I would need a vision of what should be, then be able to convince others of that vision. The vision I chose was about building a movement in the vital early learning years for *everyone's* child. In this, my most vital chapter, I would need to speak up incessantly and insistently, using the "bully pulpit" that each of us is given. I would need to inspire others. I would need to be a teacher—in words and example. I would need to convene good people to move toward common cause and collaborative relationships. I would need to exercise the power of insistent purposefulness laced throughout with decency and common sense. I would need to welcome everyone into the tent, understanding that the fullest range of perspectives and people leads to better decisions if—and this is a big *if*— there is a genuine willingness to listen (sometimes especially to those who might tell us what we might prefer not to hear).

What my children need, and their children, is what every child needs. In the words of television's gentle philosopher, the now departed Fred Rogers: "Our goal as a nation must be to make sure that *no* child is denied the chance to grow in knowledge and character from the very first years." In Mister Rogers' Neighborhood, he added, "*Every* child is welcome into the world of learning—not just a few, not just ones from certain neighborhoods *but every child.*"

The story of kindergarten illustrates that. Conceived by a German named Friedrich Froebel back in 1837, kindergarten came to America in the 1850s. Taking more than a century to be genuinely widespread, kindergarten was often opposed as unnecessary, even "anti-family." For decades, kindergarten was mostly attended by society's worst off (giving them an opportunity to catch up with other children) and society's best off (who could afford every advantage). Only when it became a "movement" on behalf of *everyone's child* did it become a full reality. Today, a high-quality kindergarten experience for all children is an expectation of every parent of every five-year-old. Kindergarten is still not "mandatory" in every state—indeed, in most states, including my own—but is there a parent of a five-year-old today who wants anything less than a high-quality kindergarten-like experience for that child?

I came to know that a real movement for school readiness can only be done on behalf of ev*eryone's* child because *all* children need the basics: Love and nurturing. Child care that engages the mind, not the warehousing that most children receive. All their shots. Real relationships with medical caregivers, not the emergency room as basic medical care. Excellent nutrition. The fullest opportunity to be safe.

Our mission must embrace what Dr. Martin Luther King Jr. spoke of—that is, "all of God's children." Too often, well-intended middle-class people in nonprofits target one deeply disadvantaged neighborhood or another, devoting extra resources that are frequently disbursed in non-holistic ways that lead to precious little progress for children. The impression so often left with others is this: "Oh, I see; it is about *those* children." But real readiness is on behalf of *everyone's* child—and *everyone's* family.

"Readiness" is *not* about children learning to read by age three, but rather about the blending of education and health and love and nurturing in the earliest years, with knowledgeable, nurturing parents front and center in their children's lives.

The imperative is moral and practical. What could be more "American" than for *every* child to have a real chance to succeed? The practical is undergirded by the research that tells us that three of every four seventeen- to twenty-four-year-old Americans cannot enter the military—cannot enter because of academic challenges, or physical challenges, or because of problems related to criminal justice or substance abuse. This, then, has become a matter of national security.

The country of my childhood has changed considerably. Today, two-thirds of women with children age five and younger work outside the home. High-quality child care has become crucial; the science tells us that a child's window of learning is wide open during those early years and never so wide again. Eighty-five percent of brain growth occurs by age three. Only genuinely brain-stimulating quality child care brings positive outcomes. Most child care is warehousing and storage. Think of the opportunity missed.

The wisest path to genuine public education reform and success would be delivering *all* children to formal school in far better shape. Children need to be "ready" in many ways—not only cognitively and physically, but also socially, emotionally, behaviorally, developmentally and, yes, spiritually. There *is* a Higher Being much higher than any of us.

I am not imagining tiny children at tiny desks with a teacher at the front of the classroom. But I do see "teachable moments" for all children in their earliest years: That sort of learning can go on in the shopping cart in a supermarket (shapes, sizes, colors), on a parent's lap, on the playground, in an early learning/child care center. Anyplace.

A superb first-grade teacher will quickly know who's really ready to learn, and who is not. That teacher knows how vital genuine investment is in real quality in the years before kindergarten. That teacher wouldn't be surprised to know of the U.S. Department of Education study of kindergarten showing that a quarter of "beginning kindergartners [are] eager to learn no more than sometimes or never, and [a third are] paying attention in class [with] similar frequency." That teacher would respect the research by the American Reading Association, telling us that if a hundred children leave first grade not really able to read, eighty-eight of them will remain poor or nonexistent readers after the fourth grade.

That teacher knows first-hand the frequent tragedy of the student who already feels like a failure. (I myself am sometimes nervous and uptight, worrying that I might fail. But I am able to muster the chutzpah to go ahead and try. I am a blend, healthily enough, of the "insecure" and the "secure.") A first grader who already feels like a "failure" is a national tragedy. Responding to that child, many teachers triage students—deciding early who's going to make it, and who is not. We should not forget President George W. Bush's wisdom about the perils of "the soft bigotry of low expectations." Too many teachers, and too many parents, don't expect enough from children.

The best teachers try to save these children. Many are not saved. Such failures must be unacceptable in a country that aspires to greatness *and* goodness. The wisest prescription for the future is investment that will bring these children in far better shape to formal school.

I spent my five months between announcement and actual retirement in January 1999 with scant attention to newspapering. My successor, Alberto Ibargüen, was fully prepared to be the right leader for the next era of the *Herald* and *El Nuevo Herald*. I needed to get out of his way. My getting out of the office immediately would give him a head start on his responsibilities, with me nearby should I be needed. That gave me time to visit places like the Yale Child Study Center and people and programs elsewhere in the country. That January, newly retired, I visited France to look at its early-schooling program and subsequently to Sweden to better understand "home visiting" (trained nurses and social workers helping pregnant women to raise children for success).

As the new year dawned, Alex Penelas, the bright and ambitious mayor of Miami-Dade County—building from conversations the two of us had—declared 1999 the "Year of the Child." He, the father then of two young children, was essential to what came to be. Progress would require real leaders and real partners. Mayor Penelas was both. Private-sector leadership would need to be at the forefront because elected leaders come and go. The mayor furnished the best sort of example of how elected leadership—taking advantage of the bully pulpit and access to resources—can make a telling difference.

Back from my learning trip to Europe, I held three public forums at Miami's Florida International University. Hundreds of people showed up to say what they thought about building an early learning movement. In each of these forums, nonprofit leaders—people who cared about children, sought to make their lives better—would stand up to say words to the effect of "I'm with you. Now if you can get my program some more money, I promise you that things will be better." I was a paid skeptic for all my journalism years, and still am. More money is almost never the right first response. Rather, we need to begin by figuring out how well we are doing with the money we already have. What really matters are genuine and measurable outcomes for children.

In May 1999, accompanied by experienced facilitators, we gathered 177 elected leaders, health and education professionals, child advocates, religious leaders, people reflecting the rainbow that is Miami—for two and a half days of offsite strategic planning, and arrived unanimously at this mission statement:

> *"Readiness for all children: To ensure that all children in Miami-Dade County have the community's attention, commitment and resources and, hence, the chance to develop intellectually, emotionally, socially and physically so that they are ready and eager to learn by the time they reach first grade."*

We agreed on a dozen ground rules. All these years later, my words then still hold up:

1. We are talking about *all* children. Not about any one segment, though realizing that the poor and disadvantaged generally have special challenges and will need extra attention and resources. This is not about *other people's children*, but about *everyone's* children.

2. Perhaps 30 percent of children start formal school way behind. Many never catch up even with all sorts

of remedial programs, becoming eventual targets for police and prosecution and prisons. How wise it would be if we invested on the front end of people's lives. Think of Greater Miami's enormous advantages, beginning with "gateway to the Americas." Think, too, of our challenges: We cannot create jobs fast enough; we have an under-skilled and under-educated population, and we have an enormous proportion of poor people.

3. You have been invited here because of your skills and ideas, your ability to think "outside the box," your power to act and influence, your strong commitment to children and families. Though we have gathered a diverse group—with diversity defined in many ways— we couldn't include everyone. Think these next two and a half days who else needs to be involved, and give me a note with those names (and phone numbers and addresses when you have them). I will make sure we follow up.

4. Our mission must be this: To build a collective vision for our children—*all* our children. That will lead toward September when Mayor Penelas will host a Children's Summit. There, with thousands of people, we will flesh out the specifics of the strategic plan we agree on these next two and a half days.

5. We, all of us, will need to "tolerate ambiguity." Allow yourself to trust the process. New information and working with different people and perspectives will seem at times chaotic and unsettling. No one knows everyone else here; we are all learning. Since the solutions depend on all of us, then all of us must be willing to seek mutual values that will that fulfill a commitment to *all* children.

6. This is not about money. There will be a temptation for people here who represent groups or institutions or nonprofits or agencies to say: "If you will just give my cause some more money, I promise you that things will

be better." We're not going to talk about money at this gathering, though eventually we must. Here, we will talk about our children (and their families), and what *they* need.

7. If we are not holistic, we will fail. Children need so much—first-rate child care, their shots, good nutrition, love and warmth, caregivers of skill—and they need it all. A focus on any one aspect can never deliver the fullness that children need to succeed. This is about health and education and nurturing—all together. This is *not* about teaching three- or four-year-olds to read; it is about making sure that children are ready— emotionally, physically, socially and intellectually—to be successful in formal school and in life.

8. We are pioneers. What we are trying to do has not been done elsewhere in any full way in the United States (though versions of this are common in Europe). We have the opportunity to be a national model of what *could* be done. There is a national tidal wave of interest in all this, and you can see it in many states and communities. Meanwhile, the Florida Legislature has just passed legislation that will call for "readiness coalitions" throughout our state. The time for "readiness" is here. (State Senate President Toni Jennings of Orlando led the legislative effort to pass what came out of the "school readiness" taskforce I chaired for Governor Chiles and Lt. Gov. Buddy MacKay, the latter being the point person on the Governor's Commission on Education. Today there are thirty "Early Learning Coalitions" covering all sixty-seven counties and furnishing oversight for the state's pre-K and subsidized child care programs.)

9. This will not be a short-term project. Indeed, to carry this out fully will take years. But it needs to start with a plan that will give us some short-term victories and successes on the way toward longer-term achievements. We must move rapidly enough for a real sense of change

and momentum, and slow enough to dig deep enough to grow real roots that can undergird enduring progress.

10. We live in a world of cell phones and all sorts of important obligations. It will be tempting for people to spend a little time here, and duck out for all sorts of "pressing" matters. But I ask you to remember that almost *nothing* could be more "urgent" than our children. Though the time we are spending together is significant, we need all of it. We must embark upon this process with a commitment to take the time with each other.

11. We need to figure out how better to inform people about all this, beginning with parents and prospective parents. Most people do *not* know how crucial these early years are. They are *entitled* to know, and figuring out how should be central to what we do.

12. Measurements and quantification and evaluation will be central to what we do. Our focus must be on outcome and results.

I closed with a quotation from John Dewey, the century-ago education reformer and philosopher: "What the best and wisest parent wants for his own child, (so) must be what the community wants for all of its children."

Three days later, we had a strategic plan, one we would vet that summer with hundreds of parents in twenty-one gatherings representing every corner of the community. We met at night to make it easier for people to attend. We furnished child care and food. We did everything in English, Spanish and Haitian Creole. At each two-hour session, we gathered participants' thoughts on the strategic plan.

In September 1999, five thousand community people—parents, community leaders, educators, doctors, child care providers, and Governor Jeb Bush—came together in the Miami Beach Convention Center for the Mayor's Children's Summit. (I raised four hundred thousand dollars in private funds to make this possible.) On that day thousands of people voted electronically on which parts of the strategic plan to take on first. We announced four major task forces to carry out those priorities: (1) Early Development and Education; (2) Child Health and Well Being; (3) Parent and Family Skills, Services and Information, and (4) Prevention and Intervention of Violence, Abuse and Neglect.

In the next two months, I began to doubt myself. What a daunting challenge, amounting to an overhaul of how we dealt with children and families. Could what we had launched turn into something *real*? By the beginning of the year 2000, I decided that however well-intended and hardworking we were, real and large-scale progress would depend on figuring out how to create real "public will" for real change. I came to think that the greatest driver of progress would be awareness on the part of parents for what their children really needed.

Every bit of my work begins with the strongest sense that parents—as a practical matter, *all* parents—love their newborns. If parents ever knew what their children were entitled to, and needed, in a society of decency and fairness, we could create a mighty army for change.

How is it, I wondered back then, that there were only seventeen *accredited* child care centers and homes in all of Miami-Dade County when there were, in fact, more than thirteen hundred *licensed* facilities? The answer seemed obvious to me: Most parents, college-educated or otherwise, simply had no idea that *accreditation* was the emblem that told them that there was real evidence within of a stimulating environment for children. (Today there are hundreds of accredited centers in Miami-Dade, generally meaning better teacher-children ratios, higher-skilled teachers, lots of books in the classroom, an evidence-based curriculum.)

I came to think in terms of "supply" and "demand." I came to believe we could never create enough "supply" of the high-quality basics until we could create the "demand" for such. While so much else good in the early childhood arena was going on in my community, while so many were engaged in the important work of building the supply of basics, I decided to focus more of my energy on building "demand." I asked six advertising agencies to compete for a significant, years-long campaign on behalf of public awareness, with the first target being parents and caregivers. We said we'd pay real money because pro bono campaigns tend to get bad print space and bad broadcast time. I raised more than two and a half million dollars for such a campaign, the biggest chunk of which came from the John S. and James L. Knight Foundation based in Miami.

In late summer 2001, we launched a multi-year campaign called Teach More/Love More, underscoring the crucial nature of "teachable moments" in the first several years of life as well as the necessity of love and nurturing in growing successful children. Television, radio, print and billboard ads helped build a demand for high-quality early childhood basics.

Simultaneously, we built partnerships with health clinics, birthing hospitals and birthing centers so that every new mother would receive, for free, high-quality, non-commercial information on how to do best by the child in the early months and years. Moms also received a baby book in three basic languages plus a library card, accompanied by a message about the crucial nature of reading with your children from the very earliest months. An eleven-times-a-year free newsletter, in three languages, offered helpful tips for parents. We put together, again in three languages, the best early childhood website in the country with highly localized information, and launched information phone lines for parents.

This was all good, but not good enough, not big enough, not enough to make a difference in enough children's lives.

What could be—would be—a truly transformative step? The answer soon came.

A Life Lesson Learned:

Journalism is about storytelling. So is a successful life. Everyone is a story. In pursuit of a better life for all children, I tell stories every day, often about just one child to make the much larger point about what all children need.

CHAPTER 13

HOW PRE-K FOR EVERYONE CAME TO BE

"America is great because she is good.
If America ceases to be good, America will cease to be great."

—Nineteenth-century author and
observer Alexis de Tocqueville

What was next was pre-K. How could we make free prekindergarten available to the parents of every four-year-old in Florida?

I could see two paths to get there; neither would be easy. In 1999, upon my retirement, I started working on this. I approached key legislators in the House and Senate, on both sides of the aisle, asking them to sponsor bills to provide pre-K for children in the most at-risk school districts. They did so, but the governor and the Florida Legislature had no appetite for such, and that was that. I had struck out.

The other possible path would be to pass a constitutional amendment.

It was a heavy lift. To get it on the ballot would take almost a half-million signatures from throughout Florida. (Volunteers standing outside grocery stores wouldn't make it happen; we would have to hire and pay professional petition-gatherers.) Assuming we could get those signatures, we'd then need to raise enough money to make the case to the voters.

I went back to Alex Penelas, parent, citizen, mayor and headed toward a United States Senate race. (A onetime boy wonder of local politics, he had been elected to the county commission before he was thirty, became mayor of the largest government in the Southeast by his mid-thirties—and was chosen "America's sexiest politician" before he was forty.) Pre-K, he thought, could be a strong statewide issue. Extrapolating from the experience in his own family—son Christopher was in a privately funded program—the mayor knew that high-quality pre-K could make a difference for tens of thousands of Florida families. Alex and his wife were seeing steady progress in Christopher's learning skills. "While Lilliam and I could afford to pay for it, we felt it was unfair that so many other kids went without because they couldn't afford it," the mayor told retired *Herald* Editor Jim Hampton, who produced a case study about the statewide pre-K-for-all campaign. The mayor agreed to raise the dollars to get it onto the ballot as a constitutional amendment. Passage would require 50 percent of the voters (plus one).

Penelas, a prodigious fund-raiser, called on his connections. He raised $1.8 million, mostly from individuals and companies who had given in his earlier campaigns. Most of that—$1.4 million—was spent on the petition drive (or about two dollars apiece for each of the 722,000 signatures collected). Most of the rest—four hundred thousand dollars—went to the campaign itself. The biggest push was in South Florida, with its big media markets and a third of the state's population. That's where we bought radio ads in English, Spanish, and Haitian Creole. If we could get 70 percent of the vote in Miami-Dade, Broward, and Palm Beach counties—and we did—then we probably were going to pass this.

On the November 5, 2002 ballot, voters read these sixty-four words in Florida Constitutional Amendment 8:

> *Every four-year-old child in Florida shall be offered a high-quality prekindergarten learning opportunity by the state no later than the 2005 school year. This voluntary early childhood development and education program shall be established according to high-quality standards and shall be free for all Florida four-year-olds without taking away funds used for existing education, health and development programs.*

Statewide, the future of children received 59.1 percent of the vote.

What came to be called VPK—that is, voluntary prekindergarten—would never have happened without the mayor (who ultimately didn't get elected as a U.S. senator). I helped raise money and made speeches, but he raised most of the money and made most of the speeches. He hired the professional petition-gatherers. The mayor and I traveled the state spreading the word. The mission was not to convert everyone to a "Yes" vote, but rather to convince when we could, and neutralize when we could not. We did both, and there was never an organized campaign against the amendment. I worked hard to get the support of Governor Jeb Bush—and did, though his support was not then robust. In later years, Jeb Bush, a man to be admired for his integrity and his commitment to serious public policy, became much more supportive on the topic of investment in early learning.

Our message throughout the campaign was this: The program is voluntary—no parent has to participate. It's free, and the money will come from already levied tax dollars. Any provider—public, private, faith-based—can join the program upon meeting statewide quality standards. (Sadly and shortsightedly, *some* private and faith-based providers— perfectly willing to take the people's money—have resisted higher standards.)

But Florida, not celebrated elsewhere as an "education state," did become one of only four states—the others being Georgia, Oklahoma and West Virginia—to offer free pre-K for all four-year-olds. Today, 175,000 Florida four-year-olds are enrolled in VPK, or more than 70 percent of all four-year-olds. The research already shows VPK is making a difference in children being prepared to succeed in school.

To get ready for the 2005–2006 school year rollout of VPK, Governor Bush asked his widely admired lieutenant governor, Toni Jennings, to lead a twenty-member task force to recommend standards that would be "high-quality" and produce real results for children. The unanimous recommendation of that task force, on which I served, was for parents to have a choice of three- and six-hour programs for their children, and mandated, within just a few years, a program where the lead teacher held a bachelor's degree in early childhood. The Legislature ended up deciding on only a three-hour program, and made the second recommendation "aspirational," meaning it never had to happen. While work clearly remains to make pre-K what the voters intended, we have the opportunity to make it better. (Had we focused only on *some* children, no matter how much sense it might have made to many, this would never have passed.)

The good news: "High-quality" pre-K is embedded in our state constitution. The not-yet-good news: We still need to make every single program and provider genuinely brain-stimulating "high-quality." The four hundred million dollars Florida spends on this program is nowhere near enough to ensure that every child is in a high-quality program. There are more than six thousand VPK providers—some superb, many good, many not. The people ought to demand that *their* tax dollars be spent only on programs that are certifiably high-quality.

More good news: Business leaders increasingly are pushing for quality early childhood programs. So are some political leaders. The Florida Council of 100, the Florida Chamber of Commerce, and the Foundation for Florida's Future are all significantly engaged now, pushing for higher quality and fuller funding. I am optimistic.

This is no time for any of us to let up.

Don't let anyone tell you we don't have the money. In the words of David Brooks, the conservative columnist of *The New York Times*: "The problem is not that America lacks resources. The problem is that they are misallocated."

We spend in this state less than twenty-five hundred dollars for a pre-K slot—and fifty thousand dollars to incarcerate a juvenile.

Now, how smart is that?

A Life Lesson Learned:

You can do almost anything if you are willing to commit yourself to what it takes. If the first path is blocked, take another, then maybe yet another.

CHAPTER 14
THE CHILDREN'S TRUST: A TWICE-TOLD TALE

"Fellow citizens, why do you turn and scrape every stone to gather wealth,and take so little care of your children to whom one day you must relinquish it all."

—Greek philosopher Socrates

Back in 1988, the year before we moved to Miami from Detroit, the people of what was then called Dade County—relabeled Miami-Dade in 1997—tried to pass a dedicated funding measure for children. Community leaders—the best known being State Attorney Janet Reno—worked hard to win a ballot initiative that would provide annual funding for children's issues.

If passed, the dollars would pay for early intervention and prevention programs to better the lives and futures of tens of thousands of children. Those to be helped were mostly poor black and Hispanic children clustered in well-known challenged neighborhoods called the likes of "East Little Havana" and "Liberty City." It wasn't the usual political campaign where money is raised for media and get-out-the-vote efforts. In fact, very little money was raised. Mostly it was good people, on the side of the angels, making the obvious point that "we need to help these people."

It failed 2-1.

That this vote could have even taken place is because of Florida's pioneering law—nothing quite like it in any other state—whose origins go back to right after World War II. In 1946, the residents of Pinellas County (St. Petersburg) voted to increase their property taxes to help children have a better chance to succeed. Called the Juvenile Welfare Board—not the sort of moniker that one would run under decades later—it was passed overwhelmingly.

In the early Eighties, the Florida Legislature decided any county could do the same provided its voters approve. Subsequently, such measures were passed in some of Florida's biggest counties (Broward, Hillsborough, and Palm Beach), a couple of medium-size counties (Martin and St. Lucie), and tiny Okeechobee. Was there a chance this could be passed in Miami-Dade? History would make one skeptical. In my county we pay commissioners six thousand dollars to watch over a seven-billion-dollar budget; the people of Miami-Dade have voted a dozen times against moving that salary to the state formula that would pay commissioners north of ninety-five thousand dollars. Yet...all my life's experience, buttressed by optimism and idealism, told me that people do care about other people's children as well as their own. I knew passage would make a measurable difference for children in our community. I also knew, of course, that Miami's 1988 experience voting for a property tax increase to help children had been overwhelmingly negative.

What could polling tell me? In my newspaper life in Detroit and Miami, we used polling frequently to help figure out what readers really wanted. I asked six firms to bid on polling to help us find out what citizens thought of a specific ballot initiative to provide resources to give children a better chance to succeed. The owner of one of those firms, the internationally known pollster Sergio Bendixen, responded: "This is a good moment for me to give back to the community. If you don't ask me to bid on this, I will do it for free." Such a deal.

What Sergio produced in early 2001 was not immediately encouraging; that polling showed we wouldn't win, were the election held then. But it did show some paths toward prevailing. For instance, from that polling came two key words—"children" and "trust," both to be incorporated in the banner under which we would march—"children" reminding people what is most important in their own lives, "trust" speaking to perhaps the greatest issue in Miami-Dade. The polling also showed that if we raised a considerable amount of money—none of it tax-deductible because it would be for a political campaign—we could make a strong case with voters and increase our chances of passage. Moreover, to give us a better chance of success, we decided to put a five-year limit on the measure. In effect we were saying, "Dear voter, try it for five years, and if you don't like it, vote it out." Most important of all, our campaign would be built on behalf of *everyone's child*.

All my work is predicated by my reading of history—and a lifelong devotion to what would be just and fair. A genuine "movement" is about *everyone*. Many children and families need significant support—some much more than others—and it is in the community's interest for them to succeed. But every parent, I can testify personally, needs help of one sort or another. We wanted citizens and voters to see The Children's Trust as about *all of us*, with programs that speak to *everyone's child*. As one example of interest in everyone, we made happen twenty-four-hour phone lines in three languages to answer parent questions—questions about child care, for example, that cross every racial, ethnic, socioeconomic boundary. We, of course, would—and should—spend most of the dollars on behalf of children who need the most help.

That the election would not take place until August 2002 would give us more than a year to raise enough money to run a significant campaign. Sergio Bendixen set the strategy. I raised the money and sold the vision.

One example of fund-raising:

Tracy and Alonzo Mourning are two of Miami's best, most giving citizens. She runs a girls mentoring program called Honey Shine. He's the former Miami Heat basketball star, an NBA Hall of Famer, and the guiding spirit behind the Overtown Youth Center. Tracy, like me, was on the board of United Way. After the end of one United Way meeting in early 2002, I asked her to sit and talk about her and her husband helping the campaign for The Children's Trust. "You need to talk to Alonzo," she said. So I did.

He and I met for dinner in Miami Beach one evening. I had never met him before. I made my best pitch, building off his and Tracy's love for and commitment to children. My pitch didn't seem to be working. With an edge in his voice, he asked: "Why should I give you money? I really don't know you." True enough. He talked about how he and Tracy had given money to the Red Cross after 9/11, and that money seemed to be used more for marketing and communications than for victims of that tragedy. That he was upset was understandable. "I need to know for sure where my money goes," he said. I didn't give up, but I also did not depart my optimistic self.

Oh, me of little faith. Within weeks came a check for ten thousand dollars from the Mournings.

In all, $743,000 was raised for that first campaign. We used print, direct mail, and broadcast media (in all three languages). One of the best moments came in a meeting with Claudia Puig, who ran four powerful Spanish-language radio stations with a large audience of older (and tax-averse) Cuban Americans. She gathered her top people—on-air and business-side— telling them, with me present: "This would be good for our community. Each of you need to figure out how you can help."

Meanwhile, many of us—among them Modesto Abety, the well-known children's advocate—spoke in every corner of the community. Most of the money was spent in the last couple of weeks when voters could concentrate on that election and this specific ballot language:

> *Shall the charter be amended to name the independent special district for children's services "The Children's Trust" with authority to:*

- *Fund improvements to children's health, development and safety.*

- *Promote parental and community responsibility for children.*

- *Levy an annual ad valorem tax not to exceed one-half mill to supplement current county expenditures for children's services. (This levy requires voter renewal in 2008.)*

- *Have membership as provided in state law for home-rule counties?*

The final tally: 67 percent favorable, exactly the reverse of what had happened back in 1988. It wasn't as though voters now loved children, and hadn't in 1988. This time, fourteen years later, they did so for five reasons:

- *One: It would be about everyone's family, everyone's child.*

- *Two: It was about trust. (That is, "I can trust you to spend my money.")*

- *Three: Most homeowners wouldn't pay much. Indeed, an owner of a median-assessed-value home, minus Florida's homestead exemption, would pay not even a dollar a week. Because there is considerable wealth—as well as poverty—in Miami-Dade, The Trust would begin with at least sixty million dollars a year to help children.*

- *Four: An independent public-private board would oversee where every dollar would go.*

- *Five: The money would provide high-quality services but never in a way to replace county commission dollars. Trust dollars, then, would need to be extra dollars for extra prevention and intervention.*

What worked? We recruited visible leaders in every corner of the community. Built a coalition reflecting the community to be served. Worked from relationships of trust built over years to raise hundreds of thousands of dollars. Didn't spend advertising money—most effectively with Spanish-language television ads starring longtime news anchor Leticia Callava—until close to Election Day, when voters would be ready to take the time to understand the issue.

With a two-thirds majority voting in favor of it, The Children's Trust came into being in 2003. We had five years to prove that we had kept the people's trust—that their dollars were being wisely used for measurably positive outcomes for children.

In the years that followed, we spent millions on incentives for higher-quality child care and after-school care, and for quality summer programs. Led by Dr. Judith Schaechter, a pediatrician with a world-class heart and mind, we invested in health teams (a nurse alongside a social worker) in more than a hundred public schools. We underwrote smaller, but very innovative programs—one example being Children of Inmates, which helps to break the cycle of incarceration. Laced throughout all the funding were initiatives to help children with special needs (one of every six children in America).

The years passed quickly. It was 2008 and time for the second Trust campaign. Over the years, I had kept the Mournings posted on what The Children's Trust was doing. In the spring of 2008, we met for lunch at a café in Coconut Grove. The conversation flowed. We talked about our families and basketball and books and Africa. (They were helping out in the aftermath of the genocide in Rwanda; I had just been to Democratic Republic of Congo.)

It was one of those conversations you don't want to end. But at some point you must ask for the money, and I did—for twenty-five thousand dollars. Alonzo Mourning said: "Make it fifty." Such moments are rare and memorable. Seldom will someone do more than you ask. "I am humbled and inspired," I said. Alonzo responded: "Please don't say that. It is we who are humbled and inspired." A week later, I had a campaign check for fifty thousand dollars.

But could we win a second campaign? The economy had changed—dramatically. Because Miami is a get-rich-quick place, it's a get-poor-quick place, too. Return with me to the Roaring Twenties and the dawn of modern Miami. History tells us that 1929 was the start of the Great Depression; here, aided by a hurricane and unsustainable real estate sales, that depression arrived three years earlier. We in Miami were "flipping houses" way before anyone else.

The election to reauthorize The Children's Trust would take place in late August 2008. A pugilistic presidential campaign—John McCain vs. Barack Obama—was underway. Property values were declining. Financial institutions were failing. Gas prices were rising. People were frightened. The Great Recession was underway. It was a lousy time to vote for a tax.

We could do nothing about the timing. It was now, or never.

This time, I raised $1,646,765 to make the case that The Children's Trust should exist in perpetuity. It took speech upon speech, phone call after phone call, letter after letter and, for most of the money, one-on-one meeting after one-on-one meeting. Making it more difficult to raise money, nothing from a contribution could be deducted from taxes. But if we won, what a return on investment! Property values already had climbed in Miami-Dade; in the next ten years, The Trust would be able to invest more than a billion dollars for early intervention and prevention. That's quite a return on an investment of less than two million dollars.

Another fund-raising moment: In 2002, I had gone to see Kirk Landon. He had run for years a major insurance company called the American Bankers Insurance Group. Then he sold the company and created a foundation (called "ABIG," playing off both the company name and Kirk's generous vision). I wanted him to give money to help The Children's Trust come to pass. No way, he said. "This strikes me as a bunch of do-gooder liberals giving away money that won't lead to much. I've a good mind to put up some money to run a campaign against this."

I made my best pitch and departed. "If you pass this, and I don't think you will," he said as I left, "let me know what you do with the money." It did pass. Over the years to come, I regularly updated him as to how the dollars were being used and what difference was being made in children's lives. Now it was 2008, time for reauthorization or oblivion for The Children's Trust. Again I called on Kirk Landon. "You were right, and I was wrong," he said. "I'm giving you fifty thousand dollars, and if you need another fifty thousand dollars during the campaign, come back." Kirk gave a hundred thousand dollars in all.

Raising money produces good moments and bad. Some could give much and do not. Others, with much less to give, give beyond expectations. You forget neither. I remember the man, very rich, who made it clear a few years hence that he wasn't going to give anything to help The Children's Movement of Florida, accompanied by the need to belittle me and my work. The best I could do was bow out graciously. It was painful.

But I prefer to remember the Kirk Landons of the tough mind and tender heart.

We had enough money now to hire Sergio Bendixen as the overall strategist, as well as a fulltime campaign manager, the experienced Susan Vodicka. Diana Ragbeer led a grassroots campaign with hundreds of community volunteers. We asked Bishop Victor Curry, with long and deep ties in the African American community, and Da-Venya Armstrong to lead a campaign that would reach the one hundred largest black churches.

We told Modesto Abety, now in charge of The Children's Trust, that his role would not be to campaign but rather to continue to keep running a high-quality organization emphasizing customer service and public service. I met with providers who received money from The Trust and told them that I would never ask them for money, but that they certainly should tell others what could be lost—tens of millions of dollars that gave nonprofits the chance to fund high-quality programs for children and their families. We enlisted the support of the community's best known—Jeb Bush, Gloria and Emilio Estefan from the music world, the Mournings, Congresswoman Ileana Ros-Lehtinen, and Florida House Speaker Marco Rubio. I did a TV commercial, too, its fundamental message being "We kept your trust."

Built from new polling and five years of Trust achievements, we had somewhat different ballot language this time:

> *Shall The Children's Trust, the independent special district for children's services, be renewed to fund improvements to children's health, development and safety, such as:*

- *Programs to reduce violence and keep children safe.*

- *After-school and summer programs.*

- *Programs to improve the educational quality of child care.*

- *Health care teams for public schools.*

- *Promote parental and community responsibility for children.*

- *Continue the annual ad valorem tax not to exceed one-half mill?*

Now came the evening of August 26, 2008. Hundreds of us gathered in the Biltmore Hotel in Coral Gables to learn whether the vital work of The Children's Trust could continue in perpetuity.

Even as the Great Recession descended, it wasn't close.

Yes: 151,203. No: 25,774.

People will make the right decisions when they have all the information. We won an astonishing 85.44 percent of the vote—85 percent of the non-Hispanic white vote, 77 percent of the Hispanic vote, 97 percent of the black vote—and prevailed in all but one of Miami-Dade's 747 precincts. (I'm still vexed about losing that last one, in the northwest corner of Miami-Dade.)

We had persuaded our fellow citizens to bestow a great gift upon *all* our children *and* reaffirmed the core of my optimistic, idealistic soul. Quoted in a subsequent case study on this election, commissioned by the W.K. Kellogg Foundation, I said: "This is what I have lived my whole life for...[the] sense that if you do good things and tell people as close to the truth as you can get and are willing to be fair, they're willing to do things."

If this could come to pass in Miami, it could be done anywhere.

A Life Lesson Learned:

Trust these days is the central issue in America. People believe in people, or do not. You have to earn trust, and keep it. People will sacrifice, pay more taxes, give more—but they have to trust you. You can lose it so easily. Keep their trust, and no telling what you can make happen.

CHAPTER 15
WHAT IT TAKES TO BUILD A REAL MOVEMENT

*"It is not beyond our power to create a world where
all children have access to a good education."*
–Nelson Mandela

Now that The Children's Trust had been passed once more—
this time with even more support than in 2002—what could
come next?

A victory celebration furnishes only momentary exhilaration.
The real joy comes in getting there. The adventure is in
making difficult things come to pass. With the overwhelming
community ratification of The Children's Trust in 2008, Sergio
Bendixen, the political strategist behind both Trust elections,
foresaw something bigger. That, he said, would be to build a
real "movement" for children.

I've often asked audiences what the Civil Rights Movement
was about. Most frequently, I will hear that it was about
black people or African Americans or minorities. Not so,
I respond; in its most meaningful way, the Civil Rights
Movement was about *all* people—an American sense of equity
for *everyone*. That is true, too, of the Women's Movement. A
"real movement" is about *all* of us. The greatest moments of
American history, beginning with the revolution that gave us a
nation, began with understanding that it is about *all of us*. You
never build a real movement—you cannot—for "*those*" people,
whomever they may be. It must be about *us*.

Hence, a real "movement" for children in Florida could only be built upon the same premise that we passed The Children's Trust in Miami-Dade County: This is about *everyone's* child. It is akin to the moral and practical purpose of good journalism—making our country and our communities a better place for *all*.

In the last quarter of 2008, subsequent to the second passage of The Trust, we were a long way from the actual beginning of The Children's Movement of Florida. Indeed, that name didn't yet exist. That fall, though, we started down the path. We knew that birthing a movement would be difficult. We knew that a real movement would need to be both sweeping *and* focused, profoundly bipartisan (working with some people you'd vote for, some you wouldn't), well-funded, and welcomed by those we wanted to help. We knew it would take extensive planning and research, real time and real effort.

We knew that children needed many things; we also knew that we could not be "for" everything and be effective. We knew we had to focus, focus, focus. We had our own ideas, but didn't know anywhere near enough about other people's ideas. What did Floridians, especially parents, believe were the most important priorities when it came to early childhood and education policy? How could we build a consensus for agreed-upon priorities to improve, measurably so, the lives and futures of children?

The year-and-a-half it took to reach the actual launch was worth every month. How we arrived there provides a possible path for other communities and other states.

In the beginning of January 2009, Sergio and I hosted citizens from throughout Florida to discuss whether there might be enough need and enough support for a statewide initiative on behalf of children. We arrived in that first meeting at a list of fifteen policy issues—too many, of course, for any genuine focus. Roberto Martinez, a former U.S. Attorney and a member of the Florida Board of Education, urged us to travel the state to gather guidance and buy-in. That was wise. We traveled to meetings in Orlando (hosted by former Lt. Gov. Jennings), Panama City (hosted by former House Speaker

Allan Bense), and Tampa (hosted by Kathleen Shanahan, then a member of the Florida Board of Education and formerly Gov. Jeb Bush's chief of staff). From those meetings emerged thirteen prominent Floridians, representing all corners of our state, who agreed to lead the next steps. Getting ready for statewide polling, we conducted eight focus groups of likely Florida voters—two in Tampa, two in Jacksonville, two in Fort Lauderdale, and two in Miami (those two in Spanish). We asked participants to rank six potential policy initiatives, which they did in this order:

> ***No. 1***—*Health care: Ensuring that every child in the state has access to an ongoing relationship with a pediatrician, well-child visits, immunizations, other preventive measures, and treatment for illnesses.*
>
> ***No. 2***—*Early intervention: Screening every child at birth and at ages two, four and six; assessing within a month every child with a suspected special need; ensuring timely access to speech, physical, or behavioral therapy.*
>
> ***No. 3***—*School year: Lengthening the school year from 180 to 220 days and the school day by two hours.*
>
> ***No. 4***—*Quality child care programs: Requiring a one-star, two-star, etc., statewide quality rating system for all child care and preschool sites, intended to substantially enhance the educational quality of these operations and help parents make informed decisions.*
>
> ***No. 5***—*Quality prekindergarten opportunities: Substantially enhancing quality standards for Florida's voluntary pre-K program by requiring associate degrees and, eventually, bachelor's degrees for classroom leaders, along with research-based curricula and quality-based accreditation.*
>
> ***No. 6***—*Parent skill-building: Offering every new parent a free skill-building program and every first-time and teen mother a home visit by a qualified pregnancy and early childhood expert.*

Taking those six choices, we polled 1,515 likely voters in Florida. To enhance credibility, and to diminish political bias, we used two polling firms—one with a history of working mostly for Republicans, the other mostly for Democrats. The results, available in August 2009, showed two issues with significant statewide support: (1) health insurance for all Florida children, and (2) accessible, affordable screening available to all parents during their children's early years to determine if there might be special needs—ranging from autism to speech and hearing challenges to attention deficit disorders—that, if treated early, might improve their children's chances to succeed in school and in life.

Polling highest in education was improving the quality of Florida's voluntary universal prekindergarten program, still lacking the sort of quality standards that would help ensure better outcomes for children.

Traveling the state to share the results, we gathered both comments and potential support. We held two-hour gatherings of twenty to thirty-five people, each steered by some of Florida's most prominent leaders—in Panama City, Tallahassee, Gainesville, Jacksonville, Boynton Beach, Port St. Lucie, Orlando, Tampa, Naples, Fort Lauderdale, and Miami.

We emerged from those sessions with abundantly enthusiastic ownership of the initiative crossing all party lines. Twenty-one people from those sessions agreed to be on a steering committee to evaluate next steps. Next, we shared what we had learned so far with one hundred and fifty child advocates, via webinar.

By this time, we had spent a year and now knew far more about the potential for a statewide initiative. In January 2010, the steering committee decided to proceed with a test case. We selected Palm Beach County with its reasonably representative mix of urban, suburban and rural neighborhoods, conservatives and liberals, wealthy and otherwise.

We called this next step the Children's Project of Palm Beach, and received significant funding from the W.K. Kellogg Foundation. Buttressed by TV commercials and newspaper ads, we put together thirty-five neighborhood and community events attended by nearly 2,000 people. We conducted surveys before we started—and afterwards, too. We learned that we had greatly increased awareness of the inadequacy of children's programs in Florida and greatly enhanced support for a statewide children's movement.

Among the findings:

- *Fifty-eight percent of registered voters believed that improving services for children should be the state's top spending priority, compared to 36 percent before the campaign began.*

- *Fifty-one percent of the county's voters answered correctly when asked how much of the human brain develops by the age of five (the correct answer is 90 percent), compared to 27 percent before the media campaign repeatedly delivered that key information.*

- *Eighty-seven percent of Palm Beach County voters said they would support a statewide Children's Movement of Florida to promote quality services for children and families, compared to sixty-one percent before the campaign began.*

Armed with all that, we went statewide. The Children's Movement of Florida was launched in August 2010 through a one-day series of news conferences conducted around the state—flying from Miami to Tampa to Orlando and finishing on the steps of the historic Capitol in Tallahassee. It got people's attention.

Several weeks later, in the muggy air of Pensacola, in Florida's far-western corner, a bunch of us boarded a big blue bus and began a month-long, 3,876-mile zigzag bus tour that took us to seventeen communities across Florida. In each city we met with editorial boards and community leaders, and hosted rallies that became known as "Milk Parties"—an intentional play on words based on the then-prominent anti-establishment Tea Parties that were flaring around the country. We carefully coordinated each event, inviting local groups of children—and their parents, teachers and other advocates. We offered entertainment. Local celebrities made special appearances. I shared our polling and our vision of a better state for children. We served milk and cookies, of course. These were, after all, Milk Parties.

In community after community, up to a thousand people showed up to be a part of this "movement" for children. By the time we finished our final rally in Key West—at the southernmost tip of Florida—we had brought together more than fifteen thousand Floridians.

Media coverage of the Milk Party tour was extensive. News stories generated from those rallies appeared on the front page (or on the local-section's front page) of almost all the major daily papers throughout the state. The Children's Movement earned supportive editorials in Florida's ten largest newspapers. The rallies were covered in dozens of television reports, including a piece broadcast nationally on CNN. We had clearly demonstrated that The Children's Movement of Florida could count on local leaders and significant support throughout the state. We had achieved real momentum toward next steps.

But we knew that a real movement could never be sustained just with rallies. We knew it would take the sort of hard work that wouldn't be seen by the public or covered in the media. We knew we had the start of a strong organization, but not yet one with sufficiently deep roots or enough meaningful relationships community by community. We knew we would have to commit, for years to come, to building enduring relationships in communities and trust among partners (new and old).

Though we had raised—and spent—more than a million dollars to launch and carry out the Milk Party tour, we knew that the real work of building something effective and sustainable would come afterwards. While we had inspired people that something much bigger was possible in each of those seventeen communities, we would have to deliver more than milk and cookies. We would need to deliver results.

Thus, we began with meetings—and a real attempt to understand, community by community, what would work best around early childhood. We were greeted with excitement—and skepticism. We listened...and learned. Meeting after meeting, we learned how our strengths as an organization could support local efforts, and, more importantly, create a statewide conversation around early learning. Without difficulty we could get people onboard who already "believed" in what we were doing. (The "usual suspects" we called them.) But engaging other folks, especially the business community, would be essential.

Building a movement is messy. Story after story comes to mind over these past years, but I share just three:

Engaging the business community has been a "throw-away" line used by children's advocates for years. Little was done to make it a reality. We knew we needed to "bring them to the table." We envisioned a couple hundred business leaders from across Florida at a lunchtime event in Tallahassee under the banner of The Children's Movement. We needed a compelling speaker, and so we engaged Dr. Pat Levitt, a nationally known neuroscientist from the University of Southern California.

To get an audience, I called three top executives who could make that happen: Dominic Calabro of Florida TaxWatch, Susan Pareigis of the Council of 100, and Mark Wilson of the Florida Chamber of Commerce. We told them: "We will pull together the program. Can you get the right people there?" Their response: "We're on it."

In early spring of 2014, more than two hundred business leaders from across Florida, plus Governor Rick Scott and key legislative leaders, gathered to hear Dr. Levitt make the case for early childhood investment—the winnowing out of unused brain synapses in a child's earliest years and the fact that most of the brain is grown in those years. Miss that all-important window, and a child can be hugely behind by the age of four. In twenty powerful minutes, built from what the brain research shows, the neuroscientist from California planted a seed in the mind of Florida's business community that has grown in ways we could not have known. That led to the creation of the Florida Chamber Foundation's Early Learning Business

Alliance and Florida's business organizations taking a much more muscular stand on children's issues.

The next story...

I've known Governor Scott for more than two decades. While running the Hospital Corporation of America (HCA), he used to come by the *Herald* to talk about the health care business. When he became Florida's governor in 2010, I was intent on finding ways for him to be bullish on early childhood—and make it fit with his campaign mantra of "jobs, jobs, jobs." (Children off to a good start in life and in school will eventually be candidates for great jobs and building businesses.) The governor and I met several times during the first couple years of his administration. One meeting in particular—at a Starbucks in Hialeah—led to something I had wanted to make happen for more than a decade.

Four of us met in that coffee shop in West Miami-Dade—the governor and a key aide, plus Vance Aloupis, my closest colleague who soon would take on a far greater role in the movement, and I. We pushed together two tables and got down to business. I made the case to the governor that he had a real opportunity to help parents do their very best by their children, helping them access resources and answer questions about their children's development—questions that would touch on how to obtain health insurance for your child, screening of potential disabilities, how to tell what good child care is, challenges with breastfeeding. I told him about the model we had created in Miami-Dade County through the support of 2-1-1 phone lines and The Children's Trust—and how parents could call at any time of the day or night, in the community's three most used languages, and be connected to trained counselors.

Maybe especially because he was a new grandfather, the governor clicked to the concept—and said he'd help. Later that fall, the governor's new budget included substantial dollars for a parent resource system. That phone-line program, Help Me Grow, now serving more than half the parents of Florida, is on its way to be available for parents in all of Florida's sixty-seven counties. One step at a time, then another, and then another.

One more story...

All children in Florida (and America) deserve a relationship with a pediatrician. But—shortsightedly—hundreds of thousands of children in Florida have been pushed to emergency rooms for primary care. We've done far too little to make health insurance available to our youngest citizens.

For the better part of five years, The Children's Movement and its partners worked to remove a "waiting period" that kept tens of thousands of "lawfully residing" immigrant children from having a medical home and accessing health care. Each year, yet another obstacle would appear. Year One: It would cost too much. (Reality: It saved the state millions.) Year Two: This is about "illegal" immigrants. (Reality: The legislation only applied to children living in Florida legally.) Year after year furnished yet another "excuse" for not doing what was right—and none of those "reasons" ever stood up.

Frustrated by the lack of progress, I asked a well-connected and thoughtful business executive in Miami to reach out to the House Speaker about the issue. That business executive—Miguel B. ("Mike") Fernandez—sent an explanatory attachment and a one-line email to the House Speaker: "Please look into this."

Lo and behold, on the first day of the 2016 legislative session, the Speaker announced that one of his priorities for that session would be to "remove the five-year waiting period" that prevented more than twenty thousand children from adequate health care. The bill moved through House committees with unanimous consent and was passed by the full chamber on a 119-0 vote. Its key elements also were passed by the Senate, and the bill was signed by Governor Scott. Now, health care is available to more than twenty thousand children in Florida who otherwise might not have access to it. A few words from the "right person" made the difference.

Progress can require thousands of people and a tour bus—or sometimes just one person reaching out. We had both. The network we built of tens of thousands of supporters throughout the state plays a significant part in building momentum around high-quality early development, care, and education. In another moment of progress, in a full collaboration with United Way organizations around the state, we have trained tutors and reached thousands of young children to help them become better readers. That program, called Reading Pals, came to be because of the generosity—in the millions of dollars—from two special people, Carol and Barney Barnett of Lakeland.

To get this far has required a long-range vision blended with purposeful energy. It also has taken a great deal of money, all raised privately—and will take more in the future. Most of all, it has taken people.

You have read about the Katchers—Jane and Jerry—and what they mean for our work. Mike Fernandez is another significant example. I met him in the early 2000s when Miami-Dade Mayor Alex Penelas asked the two of us to lead a task force on children's health insurance.

Mike Fernandez, a Cuban-American success story if ever there was one (and there are many), has bought, built, and sold two dozen companies, mostly in the health care field, and made money on all but two of them. We worked well together and became good friends. (Our first grandchild, Mary, was baptized at the Vatican; Mike liked that idea, and his and Constance's son Cristofer Miguel was baptized there a few months later.)

Several times over those years, Mike said he would like to help our work. The first opportunity came as I was raising the money for an endowed chair in early childhood education at the University of Florida (ultimately to be occupied by Dr. Patricia Snyder, one of the great national treasures in early learning academia). Mike and I had lunch one day, and I launched into my pitch. Not five minutes into that, he interrupted: "How much do you want me to give?" He would be the first contributor, and I really hadn't figured out what I ought to ask. Tumbling through my mind was this: I need to raise a million dollars plus one more dollar to be eligible for a state match of $750,000. What is too little? What is too big? Make me not seem greedy. Do not fail to ask for enough. I asked for $300,000. Two seconds couldn't have passed. "You will have the check in a week," he said.

You don't forget such moments.

Mike's generosity was helpful, too, in helping to pass The Children's Trust—twice.

But here's the best: When Mike's grandchild, Daniella, was born, her internal organs were scrambled in a life-threatening way. Daniella would need an operation. She would either go on to a full and good life or face grimmer consequences. The operation, at Miami Children's Hospital, turned out to be a great success. In joy and homage, Mike, encouraged by daughter Michelle, decided he would walk all 508 miles of El Camino de Santiago, a millennium-old world-famous pilgrimage across the top of northern Spain. He would do so in exchange for pledges, with the dollars raised going to the hospital to help those children who would not have the resources of the Fernandez family.

As he walked that route—in all sorts of weather through forests and gullies and up and down steep hills—he sent back emails that went to many in Miami and elsewhere. Mike has a talent for words, and several of us suggested he ought to turn the journey into a book. He outright rejected that idea, but later came to express only reluctance. Ultimately, he wrote me: "I'll do it if you'll shepherd it," and accompanied that message with an actual shepherd's staff. (It now resides in my office, ready if sheep ever show up.) It was never in my mind to ask Mike for a nickel for helping in the whole process—writing, editing, design, publishing. I wasn't raised to charge my friends anything.

That book, *Humbled by the Journey: Life Lessons for My Family...and Yours*, came to be. More than twenty-five thousand copies were bought.

Mike decided—over my protestations—that the proceeds would go to The Children's Movement of Florida. But there is more.

Mike invited his wife Constance, Martin Merzer (the first-rate journalist who helped him with the book), and me, the editor of the book, to spend a week with him on the last seventy-two miles of El Camino. It tested all of us, and we loved it. There was nothing luxurious about the week on the road in this sparsely populated farming country. Nights were spent in farmhouses. On the fourth night, the four of us were having dinner after a long day and many miles, wearing a loaded backpack and soaked by all-day rain. The food tasted special, and the conversation, too.

At one point Mike pulled out a piece of paper from his pocket, joked a bit about his sometimes eccentric approach to philanthropy, then began speaking about our work on behalf of children. "I've had a good year," he said. Indeed, he had—selling yet another company, this time for a profit big enough that its significance is understated by the word "significant." He said: "I want to do more. I want to help more. So I am going to make another small contribution to your foundation." We waited for what he would say next. Mike looked at that piece of paper, then looked me in the eye and said:

"Five million dollars."

Sitting next to me, Marty said quietly: "Holy crap." Overcome, I could only say, "Thank you." There are not many moments like this in life. Mike and I shook hands—not to seal any "deal"; Mike's word is all you need. We shook hands because we are bonded by friendship and our work on behalf of the future of children. What he gave would let us do even more for children.

It should be obvious by now why I have kept my optimistic soul for three-quarters of a century.

I am not going to be around forever. My successor is in place. Vance Aloupis, four decades younger than I, with new ideas and new energy and as much potential as anyone I know—and now a key lieutenant, Madeleine Thakur. That being said, a movement must be about many people.

Today, we continue to move strategically throughout the state, building support in key communities. Our vision is long-term, which is how it must be—with a specific agenda for every legislative session and, crucially, five-year goals for the well-being of children in Florida.

What we have begun will extend well past my lifetime, but the urgency is now. The opportunities—or consequences—are inevitable.

Remember that early learning center I visited years ago, the one where none of the children, ages three and four, knew what a bunny rabbit looked like. I don't want to witness that again for any child...ever. To do better by everyone's child, you will have to help. Everyone will need to help. We have within us the energy to make that happen.

A Life Lesson Learned:

The adventure of life is making the difficult, even the sometimes seemingly impossible, come to be. That requires toughness and humility—and a willingness to devote whatever it takes, even a lifetime. The goal must be both meaningful and good.

EPILOGUE

"Be ashamed to die before you have won some battle for humanity."

—Nineteenth-century public education reformer Horace Mann

I do not think I can ever "retire." Or should.

Maybe I can slow down a bit. Maybe I can say "Yes" less often. I know I will take off more time, especially so at our home in Vermont where we spend a few weeks in the summer, and where our children and their children gather for alternating Thanksgivings and Christmases. I do try to "relax," but mostly fake it.

We are not given to complaining in our family. We know we are blessed in many ways. Every human being in every family wears a mask. Behind that mask is a blend of experiences and emotions—including pain and sadness. None of us will depart this life without having experienced real pain. How we handle that pain, how we grow from that pain—that is the test for each of us.

Count your blessings. You never need to look far to find those with pain far beyond your own.

I've led blue-ribbon panels in Florida on two different child deaths—Rilya and Nubia. (Rilya received her name with the intent of signifying "Remember I Love You Always"; there is, in fact, no evidence that she was ever loved.) Both were tortured to death. I've never been in favor of the death penalty, but I could make exceptions. There is surely dysfunction in this world, but there is evil, too.

Rilya would be a young adult now. Nubia would be in high school. They deserved the years they lost, and many more.

How different their lives could have been with early learning programs that provided brain-stimulating learning. And high-quality prekindergarten. And the ability to see a doctor or nurse regularly. And families who took advantage of skill-building programs that helped people—parents and caregivers—to provide loving oversight and care. It is that vision that has led to pre-K, The Children's Trust, and The Children's Movement. Millions—literally millions—of children have benefited. We need to believe in every family and every child.

The Lawrence family has in its DNA a passion for giving and fairness and justice. We've been honored as "Family of the Year." Now, our children and their spouses are teaching our grandchildren to give. Bobbie and I couldn't be prouder.

Several times a year, Bobbie and I open our home to share good causes and good people with others in the community—perhaps for a project in Haiti, or to better understand the reality of life in Cuba, or to introduce National Merit semifinalists to the leadership of Florida A&M University.

Everyone in our family regularly reads books and newspapers. A good weekend for Bobbie and me would include a movie in quiet, cool darkness—optimistic and inspirational endings preferred. Most of our favorite television programs were long gone before we started watching—*Seinfeld*, for example. We watch the national news, supplemented by newspapers. Our week always includes at least one book—for me, mostly history and biographies; for Bobbie, more likely good fiction.

At home the room we love the most is the library. (Two millennia ago, the Roman scholar Cicero wrote about his own library: "My house seems to have had a soul added to it.") In our home you will find an emphasis on American history (particularly on our greatest president, Abraham Lincoln, whom I admire for many reasons, beginning with his capacity to grow all his life). You will find volume after volume on racism and anti-Semitism and prejudice of all sorts, biographies of great men and women, books on the countries we've visited, fiction classics (Mark Twain is a favorite because he, like Lincoln, grew all his life), and modern best-sellers. Nowadays, I most often read books on my iPad. I buy the hardcover, too, because I like being able to touch my lifelong friends—books.

I give away many books—a "Johnny Appleseed" of books, if you will. A book is an affordable, personal and meaningful gift.

When we meet, I likely will ask you, "What are you reading these days?" The more we read, the more ways we can connect with the world.

I am in two book groups. One, with Bobbie, is for people somewhere close to our age. The other, hosted at our home, is for a couple dozen people in their twenties and thirties. Most of those books are biographies and history because everyone needs to learn from people and the past. (A Yale study tells us that people who read generally live longer than those who do not. I'd like to live long enough to share more books and more wisdom.)

Bobbie and I have never been rich, but we have been prudent. We've had mortgages, but no longer. We've bought cars on time, but no longer. No longer into "possessions," we would like fewer "things." We've bought a sprinkling of art and antiquities and old maps over the years. Surrounded by such still brings us pleasure.

I probably should have been more attentive to wealth over the years, but that wasn't me. I am blessed by the opportunity to do for others every single day. My blessings begin with Roberta and our children and all in our family in whom I take such pride and love so much. I get pleasure from much, especially from those I know and from those I will meet—and, of course, the work I do.

I believe in God, in my country, in *every* child's potential. I believe we Americans can come together to "own" a portrait of what we would want for *every* child. I *know* that children—rich, poor, or in-between—deserve the same start in life.

I am a perpetually frustrated fellow. Always wondering what more I can do, wondering what more *we* can do on behalf of children, *all* children, who deserve the fullest opportunity to fulfill what God gave each of them. I think back to my own childhood, one of nine children growing up on a farm in a loving family, embarking on one career and then another, both blessed by lifelong optimism and idealism. I think of my parents and the lessons they taught us in humility and hard work, faith, and fairness. I think back on great teachers and mentors, and splendid journalists who set an example of integrity and the never-ending pursuit of truth. I think of all that I have received from my own family—their love, their patience, their belief in me. And then I think of that summer morning in Liberty City where children didn't know what a bunny rabbit looked like. That is unacceptable—for them and for our country.

There is, to be sure, so much more to do. I think of someone I mentor, my young friend Javaris growing up in the toughest neighborhood of Miami. I think of his six siblings and his mother working extra hard to do right by her children. I think of his public school principal who wants to help him succeed. Javaris and I have been many places together. I took him to his first visit ever to a bookstore; he was eleven. I think of Javaris and his mother going with Roberta and me to a gorgeously costumed production of *The Nutcracker*. I hope that Javaris will read and treasure books and have a hunger to learn all his life, and be able to see beauty and hope everywhere he goes. I wish that for every child.

The long-lived social reformer and playwright George Bernard Shaw tells us of "the true joy of life":

> *Being used for a purpose recognized by yourself as a mighty one, and being a force of nature instead of a feverish, selfish little clod of ailments and grievances, complaining the world will not devote itself to making you happy. I am of the opinion that my life belongs to the whole community, and as long as I live, it is a privilege to do for it whatever I can. I want to be thoroughly used up when I die; for the harder I work, the more I live.*

Amen and onward...

ACKNOWLEDGEMENTS

A lifetime of people made this book come to be. There was no book without them.

Family came first—none of them in journalism but all of them good editors, especially so my wife Roberta with her eagle eye and wise observations. My sisters Mary and Annetje shared memories I had forgotten.

Martin Merzer, my friend and former *Herald* colleague, is someone you ought to have on your staff if you want the best journalism. Without his help organizing and gathering the details of a life, I might not have even started the book. A year later, I had done the best I could, having edited myself over and over, supplemented by having asked a host of friends for their thoughts. Then I went to Mitchell Kaplan, the proprietor of the best book store I know—Books & Books in Coral Gables, Florida—who led me to Les Standiford, author of twenty-three books (fiction and nonfiction) and head of Florida International University's well-known creative writing program. Les pushed me hard, made me think about storytelling in ways I wouldn't have come up with by myself.

The book is better because of all of them.

INDEX

ABOUT THE AUTHOR

David Lawrence Jr., one of the country's best known journalists, retired at the age of fifty-six and subsequently became a leading national advocate for children, especially in the crucial early learning years. The retired publisher of the *Miami Herald* and the *Detroit Free Press* now chairs The Children's Movement of Florida, a citizen-led, nonpartisan movement to educate political, business and civic leaders— and parents—about the urgent need to make the well-being of children, especially in their earliest years, the state's highest priority. Married for more than a half-century, he and his wife Roberta have five children and seven grandchildren. The former president of both the American Society of Newspaper Editors and the Inter-American Press Association, he has thirteen honorary doctorates, chaired the local arrangements for the 1994 Summit of the Americas and co-founded a vocational-technical school in Haiti.